KARMA COLA

Gita Mehta was educated in India and
at Cambridge University. She has worked
on a number of television films and is the
author of the highly acclaimed *Raj*. She is
married with one son and divides her time
between India, London and New York.

Also by Gita Mehta

Raj

GITA MEHTA

KARMA COLA

Minerva

A Mandarin Paperback
KARMA COLA

First published in Great Britain 1980
by Jonathan Cape Ltd
First paperback edition published 1981
by Fontana Paperbacks
This Minerva edition published 1990
by Mandarin Paperbacks
an imprint of Reed Consumer Books Limited
Michelin House, 81 Fulham Road, London SW3 6RB
and Auckland, Melbourne, Singapore and Toronto

Reprinted 1990, 1991, 1993 (twice)

Copyright © Gita Mehta 1979
Introduction copyright © Gita Mehta 1990

Excerpts from this work first
appeared in *Harpers* magazine

A CIP catalogue record for this book
is available from the British Library
ISBN 0 7493 9069 7

Printed in Great Britain
by Cox & Wyman Ltd, Reading, Berks

INTRODUCTION

Among the letters I have received from readers of Karma Cola, the one that continues to haunt me was written by a young woman incarcerated in a home for the insane in the United States.

The writer describes herself as having been among the hundreds of thousands of Westerners who travelled to India in the belief that they would find holy men able to free them from the boredom and despair of an increasingly material world. Soon after her arrival, while walking down an Indian street, the young woman encountered a man clothed in the saffron robes of renunciation who offered to be her spiritual mentor. Delighted that enlightenment was already within her reach she became his follower, following him even unto a cave in the high Himalayas where, she was told, other spiritual gurus were waiting to initiate her in the ways of Eastern mysticism. Then her initiation began. The gurus gave her food laced with drugs. When she was incapacitated, they sexually assaulted her. For weeks she was kept a drugged sexual prisoner by her teachers, until she managed to escape and find her way back to the United States – where she was promptly hospitalized as mad. Now she was in the process of securing her release from hospital, able at last to laugh at herself. "Because," she wrote, "after reading your book I realised I should never have trusted gurus who wore Adidas running shoes."

When *Karma Cola* was first published, critics from as far afield as the United States and South America to Europe and South East Asia, reviewed it less for its merit than as an occasion to describe their own encounters with such casualties of spiritual tourism. The tales the critics told could easily have been added to the original text, further illustrations of the price paid by those who confused the profound with the banal in their attempts to levitate above reality. And yet, those days seem now an age of such innocence – when global escapism masquerading as spiritual hunger resulted at worst in individual madness, at best in a hard-won awareness that the benediction of jet-stream gurus was seldom more than skywriting, and that the mystic East, given half a chance, could teach the West a thing or two about materialism.

But even at that time, the international press was carrying lurid accounts of an event which proved to a shocked world that the sleep of reason, beyond giving birth to monsters, could end most monstrously in the Big Sleep itself. In Jonestown, on the instructions of their spiritual leader, more than a thousand people had just killed themselves by drinking cyanide mixed with the soft drink, Kool Aid: karma attained through orange-flavoured cola.

Such tragedies, from those distant days when rock and roll was still king, continue to cast a shadow over the pleasure one might take in the larger ironies of today, such as the irony in the Soviet Union – the state which most emphatically attacked religion as the opiate of the masses – where Russian members of the Hare Krishna sect now chant Hindu mantras on the streets of Moscow, citing glasnost as the reason to be accorded recognition as an official religion.

Since East and West increasingly meet under such unlikely circumstances it might be wise to remember two myths – one Eastern, one Western – which provide a caution to the human race. The Indian myth maintains we are living in the age of Kalyug, which presages the end of the world. Kalyug is characterised by speed. Speed, being the enemy of reflection, will spread fantasy with such velocity that humans, in their pursuit of escape, will ultimately destroy themselves. The Western myth, as expressed in Goethe's *Faust*, introduces the devil as a poodle, welcomed as something harmless and amusing until it turns into the implacable force that exacts damnation as the price of greed.

Who can deny that this is indeed the age of speed if the psychedelic escapisms, the mindless pursuit of chemical and religious narcosis, the greed for supernatural powers, which entered our experience with all the playfulness of a poodle only three decades ago, have already turned into a Faustian nightmare in which fundamentalist priests become bounty hunters, drug barons hold whole nations to ransom, and saffron-robed holy men now deal in arms? And could the vague spiritual longings of those recent times undergo such rapid metamorphosis unless assisted by that powerful alchemy that turns doubt into certainty, the illusion of imminent paradise promised by marketing?

An Indian journalist told me of an interview she conducted with the members of a commune who styled themselves the Stone Age Cult. This group of Westerners had given up everything to follow a large, bearded American living in India who claimed to have discovered the secret of immortality. Unfortunately, immotality had not saved him from falling prey to the temporal and he had contracted an Indian disease. While his followers waited for his recovery, the immortal one died. The Indian journalist called on the bereaved followers and found, to her surprise, that they were not in the least distraught. When she enquired after their current views on immortality, they replied that their faith in their leader's indestructibility remained intact.

"But he's dead," the bemused journalist insisted. "You cremated him yourselves."

"The master isn't dead," she was admonished. "He's being recycled."

The sages who prophesied Kalyug did warn that speed would lead to a marked preference for fantasy over reality. So if the tenor of the times suggest that we should see no reality, hear no reality, speak no reality, then perhaps a minute's silence should be observed – if only to contemplate the perils of being recycled. In India, recycling offers not the glamours of immortality but the fetters of karma that chain humans to the wheel of existence. And even the most materialistic Indian still knows that wheeling and dealing in karma can turn into the most dangerous practical joke of all.

Gita Mehta, Delhi, December 1989

I

REINVENTING THE WHEEL

I

A Brazilian and a Frenchman once invited me to visit them in their bug-infested hotel room in the walled city of Old Delhi.

The Brazilian looked into an impossibly distant horizon and intoned,

"Come tonight. Moon is full. Karma is right for looking at jewels."

People were taking their gurus where they could find them. I, an inert Indian, much admired the Brazilian for hitchhiking all the way from Rio de Janeiro to Delhi. I had no idea what he meant by either karma or jewels. But he had obvious powers of endurance. So I went.

The moon was indeed full. The hotel was on five floors, illuminated by a single light bulb, which began on the ceiling of the fifth floor, dropped past three curves of rickety wooden banister to dangle precariously between first and second floor. The actual hotel rooms were occupied by prostitutes or traveling moneylenders. The foreigners lived in barsatis, shacks on the roof terrace. Their lighting was the moon and very pretty too, after the dingy approach. The battlements of the Red Fort broke the darkness on one side, on the other the four minarets of the

3

Friday Mosque of the Moghul emperors reached for the sky.

I went from one candle-lit barsati to another, chancing upon a hypodermic event here, a séance there, until I finally found the gentlemen who had invited me to visit. The Brazilian was in coitus with his Frenchman and out of it. The Frenchman did the honors.

"Allez! Allez!" he shouted.

"Mais le Karma! Les Bijoux!" I insisted.

"Quoi? Tu es fou alors!"

He couldn't believe I was still standing there. But I was. Ready to be enlightened. Being French, he tried to clarify the situation.

"Mais, tu vois, c'est pas le temps parfait du karma. Mon ami sleeps."

I never did find out what the jewels were, but I reluctantly conceded that the Brazilian was not destined to be my guru. For him karma was atmosphere. Not the Wheel. Like the Incas, he had attached that monstrous concept to whimsy, and was pulling his toy on a string behind him across the world.

2

We were Indians but we had caught the contagions of the American Age. Speed was the essence of action, and America proved it daily.

Some say the action in India began with the opening of the Suez Canal, when the ladies from Hampshire and Wiltshire and other mythic crèches of the Empire grabbed their hunters and their prayer books and set those high-buttoned boots on the ships that would sail them to the heart of the Raj.

They were the Port Out gentry, who struggled for one hundred years to impress upon us that the most noble muscle in the human body was the sphincter, which should be kept tightly clenched at all times. By the time they returned Starboard Home, a whole sleepy continent had been trussed up in the great Victorian Straitjacket.

Others say the action began with the Boeing 707 and John F. Kennedy, when the Peace Corps kids came to dig tube wells in Indian villages without taking payment in Christian baptisms. But they were so earnest and so drab and so into three-part harmony.

A bleak future stretched before us. It looked like we wouldn't make the twentieth century unless we spent the next few generations in the progress bus, heartily singing row your boat gently down the stream, MERRILY merrily merrily . . .

Still others say the action began when that long red line of loonies came straggling in by way of Afghanistan, the Northwest Frontier, and the Punjab plains. What an entrance. Thousands and thousands of them, clashing cymbals, ringing bells, playing flutes, wearing bright colors and weird clothes, singing, dancing and speaking in tongues.

It seemed then that the war of icons was really over. On one hand there were all those statues of Queen Victoria, a grumpy old lady covered in bird droppings, and on the other, this caravanserai of libertine celebrants who were wiping away the proprieties of caste, race, and sex by sheer stoned incomprehension.

The seduction lay in the chaos. They thought they were simple. We thought they were neon. They thought we were profound. We knew we were provincial. Everybody thought everybody else was ridiculously exotic and everybody got it wrong.

Then the real action began.

3

American mass-marketing had penetrated so fast to the Indian interior that its experts were invited by our government to popularize contraceptives with the same panache.

While population control and pop culture raced hand in hand through the Indian countryside, we of the cities and the universities were getting restless too. But just when the accelerator seemed within our reach, the unthinkable happened.

The kings of rock and roll abdicated.

To Ravi Shankar and the Maharishi.

As the sitar wiped out the split-reed sax, and mantras began fouling the crystal clarity of rock and roll lyrics, millions of wild-eyed Americans turned their backs on all that amazing equipment and pointed at us screaming,

"You guys! You've got it!"

Well, talk about shabby tricks. We had been such patient wallflowers and suddenly the dance was over. Nobody wanted to shimmy. They all wanted to do the rope trick.

The lines were kept open in spite of the political static.

"Excuse me, operator, what did they say? What have we got?"

"Hello, India, my party is saying you have the Big Zero."

Mao had lost out to Maya. The revolution was dead.

So we tagged along with the Americans one more time. Not because of right thought, right speech, right action. But because of the rhythm section. Never before had the Void been pursued with such optimism and such razzle dazzle. Everyone suspected that whatever America wanted, America got.

Why not Nirvana?

4

But oh, the tedium of being from the East when everything for sale was of the East. They had promised us Arpège and given us patchouli. Into the vacuum of our unsatisfied desires the great Western marketing machine disgorged peasant skirts with hand-printed mantras, vegetable dyes, and lentil soup.

Eventually we succumbed to the fantasy that Indian goods routed through America were no longer boringly ethnic, but new and exciting accessories for the Aquarian Age. From accepting the fantasies it was a very short haul to buying them and, later and more successfully, to manufacturing them. As our home industry expands on every front, at last it is our turn to mass market.

I know an Indian boy who used to listen to rock and roll. Then he got religion. He found a guru.

One day the devotee had his hands raised in supplication when the guru said to him,

"Your watch is not accurate. Take it off and give it to me."

The boy did so. The guru examined the watch and then returned it to the devotee. The boy was about to slide it back on his wrist when he noticed that the watch had changed. Now it was not only accurate, but it also told the time in New York and

London, it had a meter for recording the depths of water, and it registered the date.

The devotee was staggered.

"How did you do that?" he asked the guru.

"You really want to know?" said his Master.

"Yes, yes, Swami, I do," exclaimed the boy.

"Look at the inscription on the back," counseled the Master.

The boy turned the watch over and found engraved on his changed and wonderful timepiece the following words·

Guru Industries, Ltd.

II

.

KARMA CRACKERS

I

I sit under the mango tree at the end of the garden at home in Delhi, next to a mound of contemporary newsprint. Fifteen years have gone by since the first freaks hit our shores, and Indian feature writers are no longer writing about drugs and hippies. They are preoccupied with silicon chips, test-tube babies and black holes. I note the trend with relief and hope that the Oriental is to be released from the burden of being either obscure or oracular.

I open the morning paper. A quick glance down Today's Engagements reveals that all bets are off.

A mere furlong due West of my mango tree, the World Conference on the Future of Mankind is about to commence at Vigyan Bhavan. Vigyan Bhavan has hosted every major international conference in the Indian capital for the last two decades, from the International Parliamentary Conference to the United Nations Conference on Trade and Development. Gatherings in its lecture rooms and august, if ugly, Convocation Hall immediately acquire the seal of Establishment seriousness. For the next five mornings it is to be home to thousands of celibates, dressed in white robes signifying purity, male and female, Indian and foreign, as well as numerous noncelibate observers and sympathizers, all come together under a huge round symbol on which is inscribed the motto:

Royalty is Purity Plus Personality.

In the afternoon the celibates will yield Vigyan Bhavan to five thousand sybarites attending the Conference of the Pacific Area Travel Association, who are in town from all over the world for the expense-account good times 'and to incidentally discuss airfares, costs, comforts, and the problem of selling India to the world.

A quarter of a mile up the road, a seven-week seminar on Kundalini meditation is being given by Swami Muktananda to a respectably international and populous gathering, who sit cross-legged and patient through the discourses on meditation and long for the Swami's shakti—the direct transmission of cosmic energy from guru to devotee.

Simultaneously, in downtown Delhi, hundreds of Children of God have surfaced from nowhere, and are imperiling everyone's good humor by raucously demanding to make love for Jesus.

The hippies are gone. This is all supposed to be over. Under my mango tree I indulge in an orgy of sober reflection.

Can it be, I enquire of a parrot who has just evacuated on my head, that this is just the beginning? Do these fantasies go beyond the marketplace, beyond your simple buying and selling of shoddy goods?

The parrot is swinging upside down on a mango branch in an exaggeratedly carefree manner.

Consider the possibility, I elaborate, that this business should be traced not to the bazaar but to the brothel.

A half-eaten mango drops on my lap.

2

The World Conference on the Future of Mankind was opened by the Vice President of India, and addressed not only by Indian yogis and brahmacharis, but also delegates from Nigeria, Rumania, Poland, Australia, South America, Germany, Britain, Canada, Indonesia, the United States, The Netherlands, France, and the United Nations. Among the speakers who addressed the Conference were Supreme Court judges, heads of philosophy departments, journalists, film stars, income-tax officials, nuclear physicists, cab·net ministers, meteorologists, and maharajahs. It was a gathering worthy of the great debates of the Cold War, except that the subject was no longer communism, for and against. This time, all these people from all over the world and from every conceivable background were discussing the meaning of karma, and the significance of moral action.

There were special workshops for different groups. On Jurists' Day the advocates general, the chief justices, the supreme court judges and even the acting president of the International Court of Justice at The Hague, as well as hundreds of lawyers, applied their minds and learning to the problem of "Truth, Justice, and Spirituality." Religious leaders including Catholic bishops, Muslim mullahs, Parsi high priests, and heads of various Indian communities discussed "Meditation and Dedication." Eminent doctors, scientists and industrialists participated in evolving a "Moral Code of Conduct for Professionals," while students debated "Moral Values and the Future of Mankind," and the ladies pondered on "Women and the Future of Mankind."

3

Swami Muktananda's camp was not as well organized as Vigyan Bhavan. His devotees were accommodated under tents. The shoes of the faithful had piled up on the main road outside the gates of the white bungalow where he was residing for the duration of the seminar, creating a traffic hazard. Inside the gates, under the tents that covered the entire three-acre lawn, people sat in meditation and expectation.

The evening treat at the seminar was a home movie of the Swami's birthday celebrations. A distinguished-looking Indian woman in a brown sari was struggling to master the intricacies of an 8-millimeter film projector. She finally managed to load it and start the film. The eighty or ninety people sitting cross-legged in a ring around the small table that supported the projector were able to hear the sound track distinctly, but they couldn't see the picture being projected onto a screen flapping from a tiny metal crucifix at one far end of the tent. Those in the immediate proximity of the screen couldn't hear any sound. In between these two privileged groups sat a couple of thousand people who couldn't see or hear anything at all. The woman in the brown sari, rather than dwell on the dilemma, just ran the movie.

The film was thirteen minutes long and showed Swami Muktananda "being felicitated by the world" on the occasion of his last birthday. The cameraman had focused mostly on the Swami's knees and bedside table. But he had managed a medium shot of the Swami sharing a couch with the smiling Bhagwan Rajneesh, king of the Tantra teachers. Both gurus were

renowned for their cosmic energy vibrations. When the image of
the teachers appeared, people shuddered with pleasure and
stretched out their hands, straining to pull the energy off the
screen and into themselves.

4

The five thousand delegates to the Pacific Area Travel
Association Conference had cornered the rooms in every major
hotel in the capital. In the streets behind the major hotels were
other hotels, pensions and flea pits providing accommodation to
a floating population of almost thirty thousand foreigners.

Some of the visitors had just hit town, restless to start the long
journey to the heart of spiritual India. Others, who had been
around a few years, were resting in Delhi from their seasonal
migrations between Goa and Katmandu. Still others had stayed
too long and were now so wasted by drugs that they couldn't drag
themselves to the streets to compete with Indian beggars for
largesse from international delegates.

Some of these younger, poorer tourists congregated for late
afternoon breakfast at the Hotel Metropole and bitched about the
rotten music.

The Hotel Metropole was accustomed to housing poor Indians
who came to Delhi in the hope of finding work. It didn't have
the means to satisfy the more sophisticated demands of the
constant turnover of foreigners. The hotel possessed one crank
up gramophone and three badly scratched 78 rpm records—
Eddie Calvert's trumpet rendition of "It's Cherry Pink and Apple
Blossom White," Paul Anka singing "Diana," and Connie
Francis belting out "Stupid Cupid."

The proprietors good-naturedly played their three records over and over again and tried to remember to keep the gramophone cranked. The ungracious clientele complained. They wanted the chart busters. The proprietors offered to play anyone else's records.

No one had the energy to explain that 78 rpm records had been collector's items for over a decade.

5

The upmarket Indian hoteliers didn't try to make India a home away from home. They set out to show that India was infinitely more glamorous than anything at home. In an explosion of invention, they invited the tour experts for a day in the country, a slice of the real India.

Air-conditioned coaches transported the delegates from their five-star hotels to a huge farm on the outskirts of Delhi. The guests were received at the gates of the farm by two men mounted on camels and dressed in the regimental uniforms of the Camel Corps of India. As the delegates entered the gates, they were greeted in the traditional manner by Indian women in colorful costumes, who splashed the visitors with rose water and pressed caste marks onto their foreheads.

Beyond the women stood elephants, with howdahs swaying on their backs. Behind the elephants were snake charmers, jugglers, puppeteers, and at every turn the five thousand international hoteliers and tour organizers were met by folk dancers from different parts of India, doing boisterous dances to the music of traveling musicians. If anyone was bored by the splendor of the reception, the hospitable host consoled them with a choice of the finest cuisines and stimulants of three continents.

"It's how I always dreamed India would be," sighed an enchanted travel expert.

6

At one morning session at the World Conference on the Future of Mankind, the English-speaking delegates in Committee Room B were discussing "Science and Spiritual Wisdom." After the third speaker, a meteorologist, had delivered his speech, an earnest American student stood up and asked,

"Sir? Isn't science leading us deeper and deeper into the possibility of total self-annihilation? All these armories, these nuclear submarines, the hunter-killer satellites, don't they prove we're all crazy?"

The meteorologist was flanked on either side by continent ladies dressed in white saris. The ladies shook their heads and smiled compassionately at the anxious youth. The meteorologist hunched closer to the microphone.

"Don't live in the shadow of death, young man," he warned. "Let us say there is a nuclear holocaust. What will it do? I shall tell you what it will do. It will cleanse the world!

"Don't you understand? We are going toward a post-nuclear, post-Armageddon *Golden Age!*"

The American student nodded sagely and sat down, grasping the moral significance of nuclear war for the first time.

And India acquired another willing convert to the philosophy of the meaningfully meaningless.

7

Or was it the meaninglessly meaningful?
Did anyone know what was happening?

"It's the shuttle," explains an Indian painter, minimalist, of course.
"We have all been buggered by the shuttle. Shuttle diplomacy. Shuttle religion. Shuttle fantasy."

And at what price?
Your reason? Your religion? Your health?

"I don't know," says a female German economist from Hamburg, on the lam in India for fear that she might become another Ulrike Meinhof if she goes home.
"But I think they should definitely have a quality control on gurus. A lot of my friends have gone mad in India."

8

The early Christian missionaries were not paranoid. Heathens do dabble in the irrational, and none more elaborately than Indian heathens, who have in their long evolution spent a couple of thousand years cultivating the transcendence of reason, another couple of thousand years on the denial of reason, and even more millennia on accepting reason but rejecting its authenticity. To be cast adrift in this whirlpool of differing views on the validity of simple mental activity seems a very high price to pay for cheap airfares.

The painter may be onto something. The speed of jet travel appears to have eliminated the distinctions between geography and philosophy. Or those between hallucination and salvation. Or those between history and mythology. Which means that although one can get anywhere, one is packing all the wrong things for simple survival, let alone for having a lovely time.

But what about us who aren't going anywhere, who sit on the dusty circus ground tapping our feet to the rhythms of the all-promising Fifties? What price do we pay for our fantasies? Our only acceptable coin seems to be piety, or our reputation for it, and we are spending it with the same reckless hilarity as those who pay in reason. We smear caste marks on the foreheads of travel agents, we turn karma into a soft option fee for a post-Armageddon utopia, and we treat home movies as an acceptable alternative to benediction.

At the height of the Nepalese Gold Rush, an Indian matinee idol showed up in Katmandu, and immediately identified the names of God with the rampant drug scene. Out of his vision came an Indian film that grossed the biggest box office receipts of that year and the next five years. The film owed three quarters of its popularity to the hit song *"Dum Maro Dum."* The literal translation of the lyrics reads,

Take a drag. Take a drag. I'm wiped out.
Say it in the morning. Say it in the evening.
Hare Krishna Hare Rama Hare Krishna Hare Rama.

The villagers who queued for the blockbuster epic were familiar with the presence of foreign religious heads who had spread throughout the land in incomprehensibly large numbers. The pilgrims were already identifiable enough to become stock comic characters in a country that has media men lamenting the impossibilities of communications.

Meanwhile the religious heads were laughing at the Indian film industry's view of the drug scene, comprising a cast of hundreds, packed together in a small wooden hut purporting to be a Nepalese discotheque, inhaling through a truly astounding collection of pipes, all shot in loving close-up through a blood-red filter.

Only a negligible amount of people, some Indian, some foreign, were surprised that the song and the film did not become an occasion for mass religious indignation. Instead the whole continent, wayside tea stalls and all, rocked on to the lyrics,

Take a drag. I'm wiped out.
Hare Krishna Hare Rama.

When you think what Elvis went through for "Hound Dog." Admittedly being a white man then was a serious and valid religion, and singing black songs was clearly satanic. But why and when had the sturdy rock and roller become the religious clown, and why were we, laughing all the way, selling our birthright for a mess of pot?

"I stopped laughing for a month," says the American designer, who has whirled with dervishes in Turkey.

"That old man with his nice white beard turned on me and said, 'Be careful how you laugh. You become what you laugh at.'

"Scared the shit out of me."

9

Reason and religion may have become the targets of popular amusement. But surely the laughter must stop when it threatens the health?

"Mademoiselle, how many French persons do you think there are in India at the present moment?" asks a French diplomat.

"Twenty thousand, thirty thousand?" I guess, erring on the side of exaggeration.

"Then you will be surprised to learn that by our calculations on the Indian subcontinent, which includes of course Afghanistan, Pakistan, and Nepal, our figures show the presence of about two hundred and thirty thousand French citizens. For these we have a record. But we calculate that there are perhaps another twenty thousand who are here without papers. Naturally we have no record of the children who may have been born to French citizens unless the parents inform us, and many do not. A lot of our people contact us only when they are ill or dying."

A quarter of a million French. That meant how many Americans, Germans, Scandinavians, Australians, Canadians, Italians, South and Central Americans, British, Swiss, and so on?

The diplomat had calculated that of the quarter million French people on the subcontinent, a good eighty percent were in pursuit of either mind expansion or obscure salvations.

"The same is true of most of the other nationals who are here in large numbers, except of course those from Russia or the Eastern Bloc countries. The true misfortune is that the numbers are increasing not decreasing despite our best efforts to teach people that things are not easy here."

In recognition of the difficulties of remaining intact in Asia, most embassies have, over the last three or four years, acquired doctors or psychiatrists or often both, whose only function is to deal with the casualties of the great pilgrimage.

For a month I tried to meet an embassy doctor, but each rendezvous was canceled as the doctor was urgently required to accompany another casualty back to the mother country. In four weeks the doctor had flown between Europe and India a dozen times. He had been attached to the Delhi Embassy for barely a month, but in that short time his feeling for those he accompanied, diseased, suffering from malnutrition, or trapped in inarticulate nightmares, had gone from sympathy to contempt to fear.

"They are scum. What is the point of taking them back home where they can infect other people with their lies and their dirty habits? I sometimes wonder why we don't let them die here in India, where it doesn't matter."

As the doctor reluctantly ferries his fellow citizens home, making sure they remain attached to their plasma and glucose drips, and doubtless in the air lanes at thirty thousand feet above sea level crosses other jets returning to India with their cargoes of illegal immigrants just as firmly attached to handcuffs, the Indian Mental Health Association publishes one of those reports that makes everyone gulp.

The Association's random surveys reveal that a large proportion of villagers living around major Indian cities suffer from high anxiety. To combat the nervous tension, many villagers in the environs of cities such as Bombay, Delhi, Agra, Benares, with their high proportion of international travelers, have become dependent on drugs. Dropping uppers and downers with the best of them. The same villagers who fifteen years ago couldn't be induced to take smallpox vaccinations because of their distrust of chemicals.

IO

Years ago a group of European travelers who used to go in and out of India illegally told me how they did it, and even how they had turned their methods to profit. They explained that the whole operation hinged on the villager's traditional hospitality.

They would turn up at a village on the Indo-Pakistan border and ask to be taken in. The guest is a god in India. If he is also a traveler and a mendicant in search of religious enlightenment, the host considers himself doubly blessed. When on top of everything he is an erstwhile sahib, the excitement is almost intolerable, and the villager feels nothing is too good for his guest. To offer to pay for the villager's hospitality would be considered an open insult to the generosity of the host. The correct method of repaying village hospitality is to share.

The travelers shared their women, a not unduly alarming phenomenon in the Indian countryside where polyandry and polygamy are often widespread. But the European girls had blonde hair and blue eyes and, like the mythological Indian Apsarasas, appeared to be forever sixteen years old. The travelers also shared their hypodermics. Inevitably the villagers got a taste for dangerous living, and the Europeans had for years used the villagers' addictions to make them active collaborators in maintaining illegal border routes.

The travelers were proud of their ingenuity. They felt they were to be admired for their egalitarian methods, which included sharing their women. They also maintained that they had performed a charitable function in helping hundreds of people, who might otherwise have found it impossible, to enter India and find their immortal souls.

What about the villagers?

"Well you can't make an omelet without breaking eggs."

At a superficial glance the land appears to be ankle deep in eggshells.

It seems reasonable to enquire whether any optimists got the omelet in their karma. And also whether karma is what it's cracked up to be.

III

BE BOP

I

It's like entering a haunted house on a dare. Especially if your motives are necromantic—going in not to seek but to find out what happens to those who don't come back.

"It's beautiful you're here," they assured me. "It's just beautiful."
I fanned my face with a clutch of lush ashram brochures.
"Poona in this heat is beautiful?" I asked, astonished.
They laughed intolerably beautiful laughs.
"No. In this SPACE. It's just beautiful."
Then they added,
"Don't stay more than a couple of days or you might end up staying here the rest of your life."

They weren't the first to warn me of the danger. Rational friends had hinted at possible perils.
"Don't tell them too much about yourself or they'll know

27

where to find you when they want to take their revenge," said an astute sophisticate. Diplomat.

"Don't look at the eclipse of the moon or your luck will go when you need it," said a tycoon. Gambler.

"Don't go alone. You'll get raped," whispered a fleshy woman. Housewife.

"Don't play the cultures babe. That's the way to madness," said a traveling man. Writer.

"Sacred knowledge in the hands of fools destroys," said the old folks. *The Upanishads.*

2

In the ashram the guru was known to be God. Some of the ashram inmates were aspiring to become God. One of them, a chubby five-year-old Helvetian, had been born God. The devotees were very proud of him.

"God calls him the Buddha," they announced. "He's a very high soul."

A ragged blond urchin was meandering down the path with a gang of fellow urchins of diverse nationalities. They seemed, in the way of children, to be preoccupied with picking up bits of string and other garbage lying on the road and stuffing these into their pockets. At one point the whole troupe came to a halt, and a fierce fight ensued over possession of a discarded bicycle tire.

I tried to *see* as well as look at the little Master ambling toward us while an ecstatic acolyte told his story.

"He wasn't born here, you know. He comes from Switzerland. When he was a two-year-old baby in Zurich he saw a photograph of God, and fell on his face in front of it. He told his father, 'You're not my Daddy. The man in that picture is my Daddy.' He kept asking to go to his Daddy; until his parents brought him right here. To Poona. We were there when he had his first darshan with God. He flung himself at God's feet shouting, 'Daddy! Daddy!' It was so moving. We all felt really humble to be present.'

A faint wave of nausea passed over me. A touch of the sun, I thought, and forced myself to concentrate.

"Well, God looked down at him and smiled. You could feel the high energy passing through them. He put his hands on the boy's shoulders and said softly, 'Welcome Enlightened One.' Then he announced, 'The Buddha has come. This child is Siddhartha.'"

The Buddha and his pals were now among us, clamoring for sweets. Formal introductions were made between the Buddha and myself.

"Where have you come from?" the Buddha asked me.

"Bombay," I replied.

"Can you buy me some guns and soldiers when you go back?" eagerly requested the Enlightened Master.

I began to laugh uncontrollably. So did the others. When we had calmed down they turned to me and asked,

"Isn't that just beautiful?"

You can't always count on your sense of the ridiculous when everyone around you is laughing too.

3

The next day I went off to hear God's morning discourse. God sat in a cushioned swivel chair with a blue denim hat on his head and spoke about the revolution. As the discourse gathered momentum it became clear that God was an intellectual snob. He dropped only the heaviest names. Jesus. Marx. Mahavira. And Fritz Perls. His two-thousand-odd devotees inhaled, writhed or listened in an ecstasy of *being*.

Present in the gathering were several Japanese and Korean disciples who spoke no English. They sat in the early morning sunlight staring at God with beatific smiles, the envy of their occidental brothers.

"They can hear with their hearts. There are no words to stand between them and God's pure energy. They can be one with him."

"Did you feel God's aura? Did you get a hit off the energy?" they demanded.

"Well, uh, he's very widely read," I backtracked, trying to get a little room.

They looked at me coldly.

"It's beautiful that you're here. But just why are you here?"

"As a tourist," I explained.

"Oh," they said, and the steel shutters came down over their eyes.

That night a dozen devotees came for dinner. Americans, French, Swedes, Scots, Midlands English, and an Indian girl from Kenya. We sat on a veranda on low wicker chairs arranged in a circle around a billiard table. Outside, the purples and magentas of the bougainvillea bushes were dulled by the heavy blackness of the night. Occasionally a nightjar would break from the bushes and shriek its way to the plane trees, which ringed the lawns.

Inside, the billiard table was presenting an impenetrable barrier to conversation. You had to stand up to see who was talking to you or bend under the table to address yourself hopefully to the right set of feet. It was a perfect example of maladroit Indian social arrangements, which always ensure that even if you start the evening razor keen on conversation, you are inexorably forced to end the evening contemplating your navel.

The foreigners, despite their many meditations, had not yet acquired the serenity that years and years of practice give the Indian. Every now and then, when the tension of inadequate communication became too much, they would leap from their wicker chairs, rush for the billiard cues, and send ivory balls careening down the green baize. On such occasions it was possible to circulate.

I marked my man, and when the moment came I took his place in a group of large, orange-robed, English and American male devotees who were in animated conversation with an American girl in civvies, a fellow houseguest.

"Where you from?" someone asked her.

"California," she replied.

"Oh yeah?"

"Yeah. You know. Cokes. Tacos. Surfing."

"How dreadful!"

"Why? Where you from?"

"Well, in my previous life I came from Essex. That's a county in England."

"And you?"

"California, babe. Just like you. Tell me more. Remind me."

"Okay. Popcorn? Jacuzzis? Redwoods?"

"Oh yeah. Oh *yes.*"

"Thousand Island dressing and rare steaks."

"No steak."

"What's wrong with good American steak?"

"Well. Like it's bad to eat dead meat."

"Yes," explains Essex. "God has not forbidden us to eat meat. What Abhimanyu here is trying to explain is that God has convinced us that it's vulgar to kill something in order to feed yourself."

"What did you call him?"

"Abhimanyu. Bhagwan—that means God—gave him that name. Mine is Yuddhistra. Over there," Essex pointed at a large maternal Swede straight out of the lead role of *I Remember Mama*, "That's Ma Saraswati."

"Oh. Wow. Far out."

"What's your name?"

"Joanie."

"JOANIE?" shouts California in disbelief. "That is really far out."

"What an odd name," says Essex.

"Guess what her name is?" California guffaws at the gathering.

People stop playing billiards. Others crane under the table to see what's going on. California holds for the comedian's dead beat. Then he throws it to them.

"Joanie!" he announces with glee.

Wild merriment from the orange dozen. Stunned silence from Joanie's Indian husband, his Indian filmmaker friend, and me.

Joanie is blushing furiously and looks about to cry. The Indians rally to her support. The filmmaker offers her a joint. The husband takes her off to their bedroom to listen to Bob Marley and the Wailers on their tape recorder. I anxiously look for a clue to this curious interlude.

This is not a first exposure to the arrogance of nomenclature. English nannies confused whole Indian dynasties by their stubborn refusal to wrap their tongues around our heathen names. The Princess Menakshi Devi would become Wendy. The noble Devinder Singh would become David. Pats and Pearls, Roses and Robins, the great Sanskrit names were casually reduced to the diminutives popular among fellow nannies on Brighton Beach. But all that was a generation ago. We were not down on our luck in Brighton. We were in India, expensively, voluntarily and intelligently, seeking release from the Wheel of Existence.

"Tell me," I enquire of Essex. "Did you really never meet anyone in England by the name of Joan?"

Essex does not reply.

"But it can't be an unfamiliar name to you," I persist. "What about Joan of Arc? Or Joan Crawford? Or Joan Baez?"

"You are fucking my mind," Essex responds freezingly.

I turn in desperation to California.

"You can't even pronounce Abhimanyu or Yuddhistra. What's wrong with the names you were born with?"

"Well . . . it's weird hearing a name like Joanie again. We've left the past behind us, see. And names, people like her and you . . . it's from that terrible world where everyone is mind-fucking everyone else. We left home to get away from that shit."

Apparently, one of the highest suicide rates in the world is enjoyed by the wives of first-generation Indians who live in Canada. If the wives don't kill themselves, their husbands knock them off. The deaths are recognized by the local authorities as an aberration of the crime passionel, sacrifices not to love, but to the climate and other things unfamiliar. Perhaps the final solution could have been avoided if some understanding rabbi,

abbot or classic scholar had assured the dislocated strangers,
"You are Diana the Huntress."
"You are Betsy Ross, Maker of Flags."
"You are St. John of the Cross."

"It's all words, words, words," says Essex with a deep sigh.
"Why can't you just sit here with us and BE? Gradually our
energies will overlap and we will understand each other without
speaking."
California nods assent.
"Yeah. You know, lady, you should join in some of our
meditations. You could learn to be silent and exist. You look like
you need it. To be. It's really a terrific high."
California winks archly. "It's better than coming."
Doubtless. Doubtless. But how will they handle going?

The servants announce dinner and we are all saved from the
possible horrors of being, silence, or overlapping energies. But
the primary nightmare is not so easily wished away. It dwarfed
the bright marble buildings in the ashram, now it looms over the
candle-lit dining table where Joanie warns me out of the side of
her mouth to steer clear of the crazies. It is rooted in a dialectic
at cross-purposes.
"What are you doing in India?"
"I am being."
"Pardon?"
"Being."
"Ah, I catch on. Being. Yes, we all be. We definitely are, no
doubt. But what are you *doing*?"
An irretrievable breakdown in communications. Sorrowful
smile meets suspicious glance in a hammerlock.
Freeze frame on a B movie.

4

At the morning discourse the guru/God opened a letter. There was a hush of expectation.

"This letter," said God, "asks why I tell jokes at my discourse."

There was a rustle of anticipation.

"Also, it asks, 'Why do you never laugh at your own jokes?'" The guru smiled. The cue was taken. Laughter from the gathering. Then silence for the cosmic information.

"Well, as to the first part of the question, I tell jokes because laughter is a great form of meditation. People have asked me why didn't Christ tell jokes? Why didn't the Buddha laugh? But they did. These great incarnations knew all there is to know about laughter. They knew that life and death, it is *all* a big joke. So I tell you, go about laughing. Laugh all the time. It is beautiful to laugh."

God swiveled in his chair.

"As for why don't I laugh at my own jokes, well . . ." and there was a meaningful pause.

"I've heard them before."

The devotees dissolved in delight.

Here's a good one.

You be Buddha, the Enlightened One.

You are Abhimanyu, who knew how to enter the circle but not how to leave.

You are the just king, Yuddhistra.

You are Saraswati, Goddess of Learning.

Nobody is Joanie anymore.

5

Such comfort appears to have prevented thousands of visitors to India from diving through death's door. But it's difficult to judge for how long. The visitors do not have that profound Indian consolation of knowing that everything and every perception is a con, and worse, a self-induced con, a view enshrined in the Hindu concept of Maya. As a result, too many visitors take the masquerade as incontrovertible fact. The gurus, their Indian hosts and fathers, don't help them to acquire the tranquility that comes from the Oriental ability to see in a plethora of contradictions a literally mind-blowing affirmation. To go from the monomania of the West to the multimania of the East is a painful business. Like a sex change. Too many visitors discover that changing their names does not inevitably lead to a change in their vital organs. More and more frequently this discovery, together with the flies and the dysentery, humiliates them unto death. Or madness.

The bad-tempered old gents who lived in the jungles of India several thousand years ago and came up with the *Upanishads* were well aware of the dangers of trying to take on what you aren't up to handling. That's why they made the curious sweat it out sometimes for years at a time before they grumpily revealed their wisdom, and also why they refused to write down their wisdom, but insisted that it be transferred verbally from teacher to pupil. There is that difference between being kicked in the teeth and reading a description of being kicked in the teeth. Some call it existential.

6

An ashram in India habitually transplants popular Californian therapies to leather-padded cells in the basement of its own premises. The father of one of the most advanced touch therapies flew in from California to visit the ashram, and judge at firsthand the sort of success his encounter-group techniques were having in an Indian religious environment.

The matriarch of the ashram—an enthusiastic middle-aged Indian woman who appeared to have survived quite easily the change in scale from the time when the guru's entire following consisted of her and a handful of other Indians, to this mass movement encompassing twenty-two nationalities and God alone knew how many therapies—told the story of the encounter-group expert's visit with only a hint of malice.

"My child, you are an Indian. It is nothing new to us that a man must rid himself of his anger if he is to understand the truth. We know how anger blinds a man. That it is fruitless energy.

"Now, in this ashram we are teaching forms of Tantra. We teach our disciples to find the roots of their own energies. So we are telling those who come to us, do not be afraid. Go toward your anger. After all, if a man is obsessed with violence, how will he have time for more important things?

"We have a meditation in the ashram where the disciples beat each other. Hai Ram, what simple pleasure they get from hitting and thrashing.

"I tell you only yesterday one boy had his wrist smashed, but he is happy and it is very beautiful. Today, poor chap, he is in the massage meditation, he is having oil rubbed over the broken parts."

When the father of touch therapies arrived at the ashram, he was asked if he would like to sit in on one of the meditations. He eagerly accepted. As a result, he found himself locked into one of the leather-padded cells with eight other people, all of them armed and in a state of spiritual excitation. He had also been given a weapon, a two-foot-long cosh made of thick wood covered with rubber padding and wrapped in green cloth, green being the Indian color of peace.

The fact that he was thus armed and had personally invented these techniques for self-realization proved to be very little defense against the mystical fervor and physical determination of the other meditators. The meditation lasted one hour, during which time the doors remained firmly barred from the outside. The ashram discourages meditation interruptus. At the end of the session, the shaken Californian savant emerged with a broken arm appropriately terrified by the demons he had unleashed.

The matriarch found the Californian's reaction, and indeed his broken arm, hilarious.

"After all, what did he expect? What is he teaching in his own Institutes? Our devotees are down there learning about themselves. They are not playing at violence, they are being violent so that they may exorcise, and tomorrow they may look in their mirrors and not fear themselves.

"But any fool knows that where there is violence there will definitely be injury. Now, poor fellow, he has a broken arm to remind him."

Sitting in India, the matriarch could afford to be complacent about the foolishness of visiting experts. But she was more circumspect about the Indians. The trick to being a successful guru is to be an Indian, but to surround yourself with increasing numbers of non-Indians. If this is impossible, then separate your Indian followers from your Western followers in mutually exclusive camps. That way, one group accepts the orgies of self-indulgence as revealed mysticism and the other group feels superior for not having been invited to attend.

An Indian, who attends both camps of the ashram by virtue of being a prince and a cosmopolite, was dismissive of the discourse in the English-speaking meditations. He assured me that the guru was more serious in Hindi.

"These people want toys. They are fascinated by sex and violence. They all want to feel alive. What does *feel* alive mean, I ask you. They are alive, aren't they? And what can India teach them except about Death?

"Bhagwan gives them games and riddles. He tells them to beat each other, make love, do whatever comes into their heads. Until they are finished with these childish pastimes, how will they have the concentration to learn about Dharma?"

Behind such contempt lies a remorseless refusal to accept responsibility for any damage done, that tranquil and implacable Eastern cruelty that lays the blame on the doer.

The matriarch of the ashram teaching encounter group therapies had answered my questions with endearing frankness.

"But Ma, suppose in one of your meditations I discover that I really enjoy violence and never want to give it up? Supposing I decide my karma is homicide?"

"Well, my dear. Some of our devotees get these mad ideas. Then we have to do something."

"What do you do?"

"Put them in the hospital, give them pills," Ma said soothingly.

"Does the ashram have its own hospital?"

"No, no, child. The city hospital, where the nurses can give them injections and tranquilizers." The matriarch paused for a moment. "Sometimes they get better and come back to us. That is very beautiful."

The suspense was becoming unbearable.

"Ma, what happens to those who don't get better?"

The matriarch laughed.

"Oh, them. We sedate them, put them on a plane and send them back to their own countries.

"That is beautiful too."

7

The gallows humor is infectious. I left after I learned about the reincarnation meditation.

Like all the most arcane techniques being taught in popular Indian ashrams, this meditation is attributed to Tibet. It being a safe bet that the Chinese are unlikely to leave Lhasa, at least in our lifetime.

The meditation involves staring in a mirror without blinking and without taking any notice of the tears that begin streaming down the cheeks. After half an hour of this, if you haven't fainted, your past lives begin to materialize in the mirror in a series of images.

The guru who teaches the technique has been at pains to point out that it is a dangerous meditation, and requires great training and self-knowledge before the devotee may safely embark on it. But he has explained this to people who are determined to outdo Houdini. So they grab the nearest mirror, bar the bedroom door, and take the first step down that long journey to their past lives, without having paused to consider the connections between past and present.

I had breakfast with a survivor ˙from this meditation. He

looked like he was in great shape after riding the shazam slalom. Unperturbed by the humidity, he had already consumed cereal, several pieces of toast, two fried eggs, and a plate of fried potatoes.

"After a while your face just melts away. You're concentrating so hard on not shutting your eyes you begin to get really dizzy."

He wiped his mouth, belched, and poured himself a cup of coffee.

"Then you begin to see pictures. You're in all the pictures yourself, but sometimes you see pictures of people you know, such as your parents, or close friends.

"It's kinda nice for your ego running a movie in which you're always the star, but it can be dynamite for some people. I personally knew one girl who went nuts doing it."

He sipped his coffee thoughtfully.

"Who knows? Maybe she was crazy anyway. See, she did the meditation with her husband. They were up in their bedroom with their mirrors, suddenly she starts going crazy, pulling her hair out by its roots and stuff. What she saw was that she had been her husband's mother in the life just before this one.

"Heavy, huh?

"She actually saw herself giving birth to him and breast-feeding him and everything. Sent her round the bend. Completely schiz. Nobody, not even the guru, could make her snap out of the guilt of how she was an incestuous mother, having children by her own son. Spooked her husband too. I think she's in a bin somewhere in the midwest now. Never learned what happened to him or the kids."

I thanked him for the coffee and got up to leave. He pulled me down.

"Hey, don't you want to know what I saw in my past?"

"Of course," I said, and sat down, acutely conscious of my bad manners.

"Well, I looked in that mirror and what I saw just about wiped me away. But it was great. It made me know I had done the right thing coming to India and staying in this ashram for four years. Wearing these dumb orange dresses."

He was momentarily overcome with emotion. He put his arms around me, smothering me in a bear hug.

"Do you know who I have been?" he bellowed, four inches past my left ear.

"Who?" I enquired, muffled in his saffron covered collar-bone.

"The Buddha's charioteer. I drove the Buddha to his destiny. Beat that!"

I couldn't so I beat it.

IV

TRICKS AND TREATS

I

It can't be complete coincidence that Asian flu and Asian thought made a mass onslaught on the world simultaneously. Consider for a moment the misfortune of those destined to endure the two-pronged attack. The Double Whammy. Spiritual and physical assault in unison.

Even Job had floundered under such conditions. Could one expect Spock's siblings, Kennedy's children, the *jeunesse d'orée* of the Now Generation to show greater resistance? While those golden bodies were at their nadir, falling like ninepins before the Bug, the East sent in the elite corps. The parapsychical paratroops. They didn't look that dangerous in their tonsures and their sandalwood beads. But they were. Huns dressed as nuns, neo-Nazis anesthetizing the world with a new nerve gas. Attar of roses.

It seemed too easy a victory and some Indians asked why. How could the Guardians of Liberty break ranks thus? America was a continent that had made a fetish out of rebellion. Its people had left town rather than succumb to the dictates of unjust despots, be they kings, priests or, latterly, the State. Yet here were their children, in the very Land of the Free, falling easy prey to men who were demanding not only complete and unquestioning obedience to their commands, but who also extracted payment for that privilege.

And what inspired tithing. The price of abject servility could vary from paying a percentage of your income to handing over your whole stash. No rebates. No refunds. No questions. An outstanding example of Taxation Without Representation. Surely such a takeover owed its success to a general debility in the host body.

Or else to the rumor that the streets of India are lined with miracles.

2

The trouble with miracles is that confusion prevents discrimination. Difficulty is encountered in separating the chaff from the gross. One school of archeologists traces the origins of Christianity to exactly this confusion.

They believe that Jesus Christ during his absence from the Bible between the ages of twelve and thirty, was in fact traveling in India. In India Jesus found a guru who taught him much about mysticism, fasting and levitation. The archeologists argue that these sixteen years of training enabled Christ to spend forty days in the wilderness without food or drink. Also, through yogic control, Christ was able to remain in the tomb for three days and nights after his crucifixion. And finally, because of the meditations he did in the tomb during his incarceration, it was a simple matter for him to levitate on Easter Sunday, a feat not really worthy of the hallelujahs with which it has been commemorated for almost two thousand years.

The archeologists are convinced that Jesus levitated his way back to India, and spent the last years of his life in the Himalayas, where he achieved *moksha*, release from the cycle of life and death, and then allowed his body to die. His followers did not burn the body but buried it, so that the place could become a place of pilgrimage as befitted the tomb of a Master who had passed beyond Karma, and because he was a Jew they built for him a tomb in the Jewish mode. The archeologists are now fanning through the mountains around the Vale of Kashmir looking for this Jewish tomb. They have forgotten, as scientists sometimes will, that the hallelujahs were sung because good had triumphed over evil, not because the body had defeated death. Still, if the tomb is found and is conclusively proved to hold the body of Christ, it will be interesting to see if the faithful fall by the wayside. Or whether they will return to the source of the teachings, the Eastern gurus.

3

A man I know went back to the gurus before the scientists succeeded in locating the tomb. He had the privilege of witnessing his Teacher raise a man from the dead.

"There's no question about it. The Master has supernatural powers. I've seen him do literally hundreds of miracles. He's always materializing things for people. Rings, watches, holy ash. You name it, if he's feeling good he'll materialize it."

The man, although an American, had lived in India for some time and was therefore only intermittently subject to those attacks of uneasiness that overcome foreigners in the presence of the supernatural. He differed from a group of diplomats with whom I once shared the pleasure of his guru's company.

The diplomats had sat on specially arranged couches in their Dior sunglasses, Hermès alligator skin handbags held in white gloves, or knees elegantly crossed in dark Savile Row suits, trembling in anticipation as the guru materialized a jeweled medallion for a newborn baby held by its parents who, like all the other Indians, were sitting on the floor.

Finally the guru rose from his leopard skin covered armchair and walked serenely over the rose petals which marked his path, toward the members of the diplomatic corps. Some of them took off their dark glasses as a sign of respect.

The guru stopped in front of the wife of an Ambassador from a Mediterranean country and enquired,

"How's leg?"

The woman stared at him uncomprehendingly.

"Leg! Leg!" said the Master, pointing at her knees. The woman pulled her skirt down quickly, thinking she had perhaps offended the guru's well-known insistence on womanly modesty. The Master smiled.

"Gives no more pain?"

"It has never given any pain," said the Ambassador's wife frigidly, and retired from the lists of the miracle seekers. The Master looked at her knowingly.

"Leg will be better now."

The guru raised his hands solemnly over the seated diplomats and walked toward an elderly Ambassador sitting in solitary splendor on a dainty dining room chair. The Ambassador straightened up, the guru loomed over him turning his raised hands in little circular motions.

"Want Holy Hash?" the guru enquired conversationally.

The elderly diplomat shrank back in his chair. From nowhere the guru produced a fistful of ash. He thrust this at the old man.

"Here. Eat. Twice a day. You will feel well."

The Ambassador was in one of those diplomatic quandaries so

often endured by men accredited to Third World countries. He struggled to rise to the occasion. Reluctantly he put out a slightly shaking, beautifully manicured left hand. The Indians gasped in shock at the insult. The old Ambassador had in his tension forgotten that the left hand is used for ablutions and is therefore considered by many conservatives to be unclean. The guru reached down and gently picked up the man's right hand, pressing the holy ash into it.

The diplomat opened his mouth to say thank you. The puckish guru seized the opportunity to drop the last few grains of ash into the man's upturned open mouth.

"Swallow, son, swallow. Holy Hash. You will be well."

4

The way the American's story goes he had been this guru's disciple for two years. In that time the Master was constantly surrounded by people begging for help and divine intercessions with destiny. The Master acquiesced according to the promptings of his own inscrutable logic.

One day the American disciple was with the Master when He was besieged by all the members, save one, of a large joint Indian family. The absent member was dead, and had been for three days. Kept on ice in the Madras City Morgue while the family handled the cremation details. But the family, instead of organizing the ceremonies for a decent send-off, were in fact here with the Master, pleading that the passing on of son/father/brother/uncle/in-law/nephew had been precipitate. The man's life, according to the calculations of the astrologers, the priests, and the family doctor, had been cut short untimely. Could the

Master please correct this alarming discrepancy in dates and raise the beloved absentee from the dead?

The American was skeptical that the Master would accede to such an outrageous demand, or that He could even pull it off. But the Master set off in the direction of the deceased, followed by a large crowd of assorted believers, disbelievers, and bereaved.

At the morgue confusion reigned. Government machinery is not, after all, equipped to deal with the unexpected. If this occasion was successful it might give rise to an epidemic of resurrections. Morgues all over the country might be deluged with bodies in a state of suspended death, awaiting the favors of passing gurus.

While these considerations were preoccupying the senior officers, the junior staff was experiencing a technical hitch. They could not find the body. Unlike their bureaucratic bosses, the junior morgue attendants were not morbidly concerned with precedent. They were full of good will and offered to produce another stiff for the happy event. The joint family was aghast. They didn't want someone else's nephew.

But the Master saved the day. He stepped into the inner recesses of the morgue, located the correct body and proceeded to raise it from the dead.

The American is fuzzy on the details of the miracle.

"There was so much noise, people were going crazy all around me. But I think the life-force came back from the toes. You know, knee bone to the thighbone and then connected with the hipbone. When it finally reached the brain the guy sat up like Frankenstein's monster. We were paralyzed with terror."

Terror gave way to awe, awe changed to joy, and everyone fell at the feet of the miracle-worker acknowledging him as God. The Master left laughing.

"Was that the greatest miracle you saw in India? Your guru raising a man from the dead?"

"No man, the real gurus in India do that sort of thing every day of the week. I didn't think raising a guy from the dead was such a big deal after I'd been around India a couple of years."

"What was a big deal? Did you think anything was a miracle?"

The American had thought a long time before he answered that question.

"Yeah, I saw a miracle. You should have seen that morgue, guys rushing all over the place, clerks, morgue attendants, administrators. Nobody knew where anything was.

"I reckon the real miracle was when the Master *found* that body. The rest was peanuts."

5

Those who have dealt with the bureaucracy or lost their baggage in an airline terminal will agree. In this day and age the mystery lies in the heart of the Machine. Locate its pulse and all miracles come within reach.

In the halcyon days when the Machine was bright and shiny no one was looking for the pulse. Everyone was enjoying the performance. Music was being linked to pictures, the holograph had replaced the ghost.

Later it was the malfunction that carried the magic. The melted frame in the film projector was an occasion for general rejoicing. Since the West was famed for its technological efficiency we were somewhat nonplussed by this new low-quality pleasure. Our machines were the product of ingenious saving, scavenging and smuggling. We were wary of the wallop packed by the contact high, which might make us want to be machine wreckers too.

The media shamans had us in a bind. We didn't want to believe them when they told us,

"The Quality bag is declassé. You gotta release yourself from all this gadgetry."

We didn't want to engage in their discussions—if it worked, did it work well enough to blow the fuses? If it didn't work, was it better? It seemed those riddles were better addressed to Western wealthies who could always get more toys on the installment plan. For us these were not toys, they were miracles. Fortunately, destruction was only a recurrent passing phase.

Instead the pathfinders decided to marry the two kinds of miracles, eastern and occidental, for the advancement of man.

6

A blue-eyed babe stares at Naresh across the candles at an intimate supper for two in Delhi. She came to India for enlightenment, *sadhana*, but she's getting an old-fashioned run of the mill seduction. Naresh still likes black-and-white movies, wine, roses, and lace negligee sex.

Blue Eyes is from California and is the only person on the planet to offer a degree course in Inner Environments. She meets a lot of academics from Stanford University who tell her about their experiments.

Blue Eyes: It's just terrible. They got these two men—who are gay actually. I think gays are supposed to be better subjects or something—and they trained them to leave their bodies. It worked. They left their bodies in California and went to Boston with their minds.

Naresh: What's the big idea? Why are the Americans training homosexuals to fly?

Blue Eyes: This is going to spook you.

      So they can penetrate into Russia.

      See, they've got this top secret hush-hush operation, it's like a CIA cell in Boston. The gays were programmed to bring back the code names of the spies. But they brought back their real-life nicknames too. Doesn't that wipe you out?

      And you know what?

Naresh: What?

Blue Eyes: They brought back the plans for the wiring and the plumbing too, for godssake.

Silence over the sauterne. Naresh looks at Blue Eyes speculatively and wonders if he will be in physical danger if he persists in the seduction. Blue Eyes, unaware of the stir she's creating, goes headlong on.

Blue Eyes: It's not so wild really. They got the ideas from India. Look at the Maharishi. He's offering these courses in levitation in Switzerland. You've heard all about them haven't you?

      My friends are going in Jumbo loads to his ashram. I may go myself. I know how meaningful these retreats can be. When you get back in touch with yourself and the mysterious forces of the Universe. It's like all to do with rediscovering your inner environments and your outer aura and Supreme Shanti.

Naresh isn't tracking her anymore. She's in orbit. He's heading for a Black Hole.

Blue Eyes: You know what we do when we have parties in California nowadays?

Naresh shakes his head weakly.

Blue Eyes: At the end of the party when people are getting
a little bored, we send out for the Transcendental Meditation heads, the ones who've done the
advanced course in the Maharishi's Swiss ashram, and we watch them lift off.

Costs fifteen hundred dollars if they make
the levitation. Or you get your money back.

7

In an era where today's miracle becomes tomorrow's toy, it is
inevitable that the world should draw closer to the Indian view
that the miracle lies in the eye of the beholder.

Beneath the pavements of busy Manhattan is a basement
consecrated to the religions of one hundred and ten countries. It
is indisputably the high temple of religious egalitarianism, an
Acropolis for the Aquarian Age. I was invited to a sort of séance
in this cellar.

We were met at the doors of the temple by elderly Eastern
European ladies dressed in saris and waving joss sticks. The guru
was standing inside the temple in front of a fine marble slab on
which were entwined the Star of David, the Crescent of Islam,
and a Crucifix. This tableau of the mutually exclusive had no
doubt escaped the attention of the warring delegates at the
United Nations building up the road, who might have wanted to
make something of it. But we of the spiritual underworld were
moved by the religious Esperanto, this mummery of the devout.

The guru, a nice clean Brahmin, who was reputed to have
miraculous healing powers, stood in front of the marble slab in

freshly laundered robes, meditating. It was the unusual form of his meditation that had attracted many of his devotees. At that time the trend setters of the New York hypochondriac set had located the eyeball as the focal point of all distress, physical and spiritual. If the eyes ached it was significant, and many people had framed Tibetan eye charts hanging on the walls of their apartments. The fact that no one could read them was incidental.

As our eyes became accustomed to the gloom, we were able to see the guru more clearly. But he wasn't looking at us. He had his hands folded serenely over his belly and was rolling his eyeballs. We bowed our heads. After half an hour of bowed head I got restless and sneaked a glance to see how the faithful were getting on. To my surprise the faithful were emulating the guru, following his eyeballs with their own. Apparently, twice a week these sophisticated urbanites would shed their brushed denims for badly tied saris and come and roll their eyeballs at each other for an hour, in deadly earnest. True believers, convinced that if they rolled their eyes long enough they would like the guru, acquire healing powers.

The meditation of the devotees came to an abrupt halt when the elderly ladies rose to their feet and initiated the procession. This entailed sliding through the pews, walking in single file to the Teacher, touching his feet and receiving his blessing, which the Teacher delivered with his hands while his eyes continued to careen in an otherwise motionless face. Having been blessed, we filed past the ladies who were dispensing the guru's darshan from a box of Swiss chocolates. We each got a chocolate, and filed back to our seats.

It was now administration time. Notices were produced and functionaries read them out. How much money had been collected last week. The arrangements in Florida for the guru's two-week Thanksgiving Season Retreat. Who was to stay behind for a private audience with the guru. A recipe from one of the devotees for vegetarian cutlets. The sort of details that preoccupy any religious community.

Then came the moment for the guru to give us his benediction and some thoughts to sustain us over the coming week. There was a demure rustle of expectation in the audience. This was the only time the guru spoke and it was essential not to miss a word, for the road was a rocky one, out there in Manhattan.

The Teacher's written speech, which would the next day be cyclostyled and available for purchase, was held up for him by the senior-most Eastern European elderly. The guru's eyeballs began their descent. The pupils constricted. The Teacher tried to zero in on the paper. It would have been an optical miracle if he had been able to read after rolling his eyes for an hour. But he didn't pull off.

The guru's powers were sometimes limited to controlling the bodies of others, but not his own.

8

A large number of gurus do have control over their bodies. Some get irritated if their control occasions too much curiosity. They are considered the truly holy, men who refuse to make caricatures out of the quest.

There is such a man in Rishikesh, who lies outside a temple on a bed made of nails and bits of jagged steel. He is naked, his body is covered with the ascetic's ash, his hair is matted with dirt. On a broken slate propped up on a brick next to his head are written the words in English and in Hindi:

Yes, I am a sadhu. Yes, I have not spoken for twelve years. Yes, my body still feels some pain and some discomfort. Please leave me alone to meditate on the Universal Absolute.

The control of the true sadhu should extend not only over the body's capacity to endure pain, but also over its capacity for pleasure. The object of gaining control is not suppression but transcendence. Indian family magazines have on occasion featured photographs of some holy man in a stance of other-worldliness, looking into the middle distance while a huge stone dangles from his erect priapus. To the ordinary Hindu such a photograph is an illustration of a sadhu showing he has risen above one kind of impotence. The Hindu believes that impotence comes in a hundred different forms, and of these the impotence brought on by sexual desire is only a malady in a minor key.

9

An American learned of a sadhu's sexual control during his stay in Benares. The American was a scriptwriter who had left the fleshpots of Hollywood to wrestle with his uncontrollable sex drive in India. He was tired of sex. He was tired of the monotonous regularity with which his body demanded it. He was tired of sexual symbolism, starlets with golden bodies, *double entendres*, and phallic obsessions. He had decided to give it all up, like smoking. But he didn't think he had enough strength of character. He put his dilemma to a sadhu meditating on the banks of the Ganges.

The sun was setting over the holy river. It was the hour of *aarti* when the gods are praised with fire and incense. Across Benares the devout were ringing bells in front of family altars or in the courtyards of the great temples. The American listened to the bells and watched the smoke from a distant funeral pyre rise toward the crimson sky. He debated on how best to start a conversation with the sadhu.

"Excuse me, sir," he said finally. "Do you speak English?"

The sadhu who was buried in mud up to the waist, turned his naked upper torso to look at the American.

"I do. I was once a doctor of medicine."

"Were you really? A practicing doctor?" asked the American enthusiastically.

"Why are you getting excited?" asked the sadhu coldly. "Is there something strange in tending to the human body?" He turned his torso back to its original position.

The American struggled to recapture the sadhu's interest.

"I meant no offense, sir. None at all. I asked because I have a problem I wish to discuss with a Hindu holy man. You're the very first sadhu I've ever spoken to."

The holy man remained still, rigidly facing away from the American.

"No. You misunderstand me, sir," the American said anxiously. "You see, my problem concerns the body. The fact that you are a doctor as well as a holy man, don't you see? It was destined that I should speak to you. It must be karma."

The sadhu stiffened at the American's last statement.

"Do not use words you don't understand," said the sadhu severely. "You will be cursed if you do."

"What the hell," shrugged the American. "I'm doomed already. Cursed to spend the rest of my days trying to get laid, the rest of my nights getting laid."

There was a brief silence. The sadhu addressed his question to the river.

"What is this man talking about?"

"I'm talking about sex, doctor holy man. Don't you remember what that is?"

"Sex? So that is what disturbs you," said the sadhu to the river.

"Yes, that is what disturbs me," confirmed the American.

The sadhu rose slowly to his feet. He shook the mud off his body and walked toward the American.

"You wish some control over your body?"

The American nodded dumbly. The sadhu seated himself in the lotus position next to the American. The sun had set, reddening the sadhu's skin with afterglow. The holy man spoke as if in incantation.

"Desire is the seat of all confusion, my son. It clouds the reason. It produces the immoderate response. The body is exhausted unnecessarily. Watch me and learn."

And the naked fakir revealed himself in the *phallus rampant*. The sadhu applied an ash-covered left hand to its relief and discoursed on.

"Are you perhaps from America? I have noticed that such things are an obsession in that country. But do not worry. Yours is not a rare condition. The world over people are enslaved by sex. This enslavement leads to your childish complaints. See the excited condition of my body. See the motions of my left hand. Yet I sit here calmly, concentrating on your problems."

The American was frozen in disbelief and embarrassment. The sadhu continued.

"Learn this from India if you learn nothing else, my son. The flesh is only the battlefield. Wars are won by the soul. The mature man seeks to understand his nature until he understands Nature."

And the astounded American found himself bathed in the sadhu's insouciant sexual control.

Later, in Los Angeles, the American cites his experience as the sort of miracle you can come across in India.

V

WHAT YOU SEE IS WHAT YOU ARE

I

The poet said I'll buy you lunch. He was a Sikh from a heavily decorated military family, but he was no killer. He grew apples in a small village high up in the Himalayas, and wintered on beaches near Bombay.

We moved through air-conditioned corridors with marble mosaic floors and jewelry shops. Once we stopped to admire an enameled Moghul elephant, drawn by the insistent brilliance of its enormous ruby eyes. Out into the hotel foyer, past the fountains and the archways, then the humidity of the open air, moving past the swimming pool with its turbaned waiters and bikini clad tourists, and through the gray stone hotel gates. On our right a glimpse of the Indian Ocean and the distant shadow of the island that guards the mighty three headed Shiva, on our left an alley of Chinese restaurants. Down the alley and through the doorway of the Irani café with its boldly lettered advertisement on the cross beam:

Rice Plate Ready Trust In God.

We hovered just inside the doorway, blinded by the sudden darkness. The poet adjusted first, located two empty chairs at a table for four, and we sat down. Opposite the poet two small

63

blond children were bouncing up and down on a tin chair. The little girl, maybe three years old, had silver bells on her ankles. She shook her feet noisily as she climbed onto the table. We peered at the menu stuck under the scratched green glass, which covered the table. The poet ordered for both of us, then rolled a cigarette and offered it to me over the little girl's back. The little girl was getting sick all over the glass-covered menu.

"Lucky we decided to order early," said the poet to cover the confusion.

"Jeez, I'm sorry," said a gentle, tired voice. "Devi, sit down until your mother gets back. Get off the table and let me clean it." A startlingly white hand with long, elegant fingers was ineffectually dabbing at the mess with a filthy green scarf.

The man was in his early thirties, an American. His greasy hair fell to his thin shoulders. He was dressed in loose linen pajamas and a sleeveless Indian vest. His bare arms and chest were pockmarked with angry red marks left by bedbugs. He had the face of a saint, eyeballs fallen three inches backwards into hollow sockets, no flesh on the cheekbones, lines of pain around the mouth.

The poet was still observing the social niceties.

"Have you been in our country long?" he asked.

"'Bout twelve years," said the man.

"That's a very long time," said the poet. "You must like it here."

"I guess," said the man noncommittally, and stroked the little girl's forehead.

Two tin plates heaped with fish curry were banged down in front of us. Another tin plate with a single slice of sour bread was put in front of the American. The poet slid one plate of curry toward him. The American nodded his thanks.

"The fact is I didn't really come here to get here. I sort of drifted here to get away from there." The American had mopped

64

up the last of the curry with his bread and was now sitting back in his chair smoking a cigarette the poet had rolled for him.

"Just another draft dodger I guess. Didn't want to freeze my ass off in Canada, came to India instead. I go back to the States every year for a while. Just to check whether I could live there, I mean like anywhere in America. Each year I come back to India quicker."

At the counter a young couple were abusing the pasty-faced Iranian proprietor in alternate French and German. The Iranian was staring at them contemptuously as he waved a bill in their faces. Behind him was a wooden counter on which were displayed boiled eggs, bottled pickles, cans of tinned fruit. Above the counter, on the wall, hung a garlanded portrait of the Shah of Iran and the Shahbanou, who smiled with fixed graciousness as a cockroach walked sedately over their faces.

The children screamed and scrambled out from under the table.

"A huge rat just ran over Devi's arm!" shouted the boy. The children went to each table in the café importantly announcing that there was a huge rat in the room. Nobody paid them any attention. The American glanced around him and said bitterly,

"I don't know who any of these people *are* anymore. They can't be humans. Have you looked into their eyes? They're all dead, man."

I looked at the faces grouped around the tin tables with dirty glass tops, lit by daylight soiled in its passage through the grimy fly-covered bars on two small windows. More sunken eyes, hollow cheekbones. Angular bodies, limp with exhaustion, despair, or maybe just the humidity, hooked over collapsible tin chairs. A photographer once described India as bad for landscapes, unparalleled for faces. Here were faces from all over the world, drained by the Indian landscape into the same strong outlines, the same weariness that made Indian faces the portraitist's delight. What were they doing so far from antisepsis in a world of cockroaches and huge rats? I didn't think their eyes were any deader than the American's. Or even ours.

The children were holding on to a matronly blonde woman who pushed her way past the argument at the counter, navigated the children aggressively between the other tables and reached us.

"This is Jasmine." The American smiled his tired smile. "She used to be a hippy."

Jasmine sat down and lifted both children onto her ample lap.

"What the hell do you mean, used to be? I still am. One of the originals, not like all these creeps sitting in here." She looked around her in disgust.

The American covered his eyes with his hands and said to no one in particular,

"I got to find someone to talk to pretty soon or I'm sunk."

He stood up. His eyes were bleak with loneliness.

"Listen, thanks." He raised his hand in a half salute and without completing the gesture or dropping his hand he wandered out of the café.

Jasmine watched him leave.

"There goes Mike, another good one, freaked by all the people. He thought he left them behind in America. He just got suckered, that's all."

She turned to us.

"We discovered these places, Afghanistan, Nepal, Goa. When we arrived everybody loved us. Now the whole damn world is on the trail we opened up, and the same people who loved us, fucking hate us. There's too many of them." Her wide gesture took in everyone in the café.

"They're not in the same *class* as those of us who got here first."

2

Exploration appears to be a hazardous undertaking. Columbus discovered America looking for India. The Beatles discovered India escaping from America. Both journeys were exhausting and it could be argued that the Beatles encountered no fewer monsters on their way. The leviathans of the deep were perhaps less frightening than the grotesques spawned by public relations. A large body of conservative opinion held that the public should stop relating altogether if its intimacies led to such by-products as plaster casters, geriatric groupies, and preteen suicidees.

Those four loveable moppets in search of an audience began to look a paler shade of white as they realized that the audience had all along been in search of four loveable moppets. Being Merseyside naives, they had not sat with their backs to the wall nor kept an eye on their line of retreat. Fortunately for them it was the East to the rescue. Hey, Tonto, and in rode the Indians.

It was fitting that the Beatles raised the cry Eastward Ho. The gentlemen of the Empire had left their visiting cards three hundred years ago, and their great-grandsons could now at last afford to be indiscreet and dabble in the murky waters of Indian thought. This time the Britons came not as merchants or soldiers or bureaucrats. This time their entrance was more like the stately tread of the Indian caste system.

Earlier in the century the Brahmins of Western intellectual thought had paved the way. Aldous Huxley had struggled with Vedanta and dared to expand his mind. William Butler Yeats, while collaborating on a translation of *The Upanishads* had found "in that East something ancestral in ourselves, something we must bring into the light." These were the thoughts of the highest caste, the scholar, deliberating on language, meaning and despair.

Now it was the turn of the populists, the Beatles and the Rolling Stones to become pacemakers for a faltering Western heart, and they achieved a more striking success.

People are apt to follow their heroes rather than their scholars, and follow they did, rushing for mantras, applauding Buddhism in films devoted entirely to receding naked bottoms. While Yeats and Huxley might have missed the hot connection between the Void and the Buttock, the Kshatriyas, or knights, of the movement didn't even falter. Moreover they had the blessings of gurus who assured them that eternity was a cinch and the way was easy.

That first wave of disciples was really top drawer. They were the nobles of the meritocracy and they were looking good. The women were models, the men were stars, and the massage was the message. When they came out of their spiritual retreats draped in homespun, they glowed with vegetarian good health. They were unbeatable advertisements for the healing powers of India, illustrations that beauty is not just infra-soul, but also skin deep. It was inevitable that those who pursued the goal of eternal youth would follow in their wake, eager to use the unguents of the spirit if these provided the immortal complexion.

The soft sell pulled them in. Hard graft kept them there. The new society immediately acquired its Vaishyas to trade on the increased expectations of their colleagues. The traders offered cut-price tours to India with names spanning all seven chakras of human possibility. They patched together the broken ivory bangles of Hindu widows with silver ornaments and sold them to the travelers. They discovered the yoni and the lingam shapes of the mortar and pestle, and soon everyone was grinding sex into their spices. They handed on the names of holy men and hospices and sold the clothes appropriate to every occasion.

And when the trade routes were well established, there followed the new untouchables, the *anciennes royales*. Dispossessed monarchs, some related to every regent in Europe, as well as Counts, Dukes, and Ladies—nobles all, with no fields of gold on which to parade their heredity.

Perhaps it was too much to hope that the Beatles, who had scaled the heights of the sensational, would settle for the jolly lobotomies of Rishikesh, but they had performed their task. The young'uns were now open to every sadhu's every suggestion. And the sadhus found themselves falling into the same trap as the moppets. The heady excitement of passing off any stray thought as wisdom. The wild adulation. The fan clubs. There was, of course, always the profits, which moved one guru to remark, .

"Religion is not for the poor."

But around the corner were the same gargantuan appetites that had terrified the Beatles—the audience, waiting for the ceremony of blood. Wiser Indian gurus would have been well advised to remember Allen Ginsberg's brief fling at being a guru in India.

3

Ginsberg, a self-proclaimed Dharma Bum, had seen the best minds of his generation screaming for release from the American Dream. Presumably this spiritual bedlam led him to take a sabbatical in the city of Calcutta. To most Indians this would seem an eccentric if not wholly mad decision. Calcutta is not famed for its serenity.

The poet had his reasons. Calcutta, he announced, is the most liberated city in the world. The people have no hang-ups. They go around naked. It was a characteristically original view. No one before had suggested to the natives that their destitution was a sign of advance. But the Bengali residents of Calcutta love novelty and are predisposed to regard poets of all persuasions with favor.

Those were the days when everything was in flux. There were rumors about Tab Hunter. Elvis Presley had just made a movie with a scene set in a whorehouse. Now a famous, published, avant-garde American poet had looked upon India and pronounced it free. Naturally Calcutta thought his reference was to the carnal. Before you could say snap, the Beat prophet was encircled by *vers libres* satyrs.

People started arriving from miles around in delicious anticipation of an orgy. You needed a ticket to ride, but in those early days it wasn't the donation of a month's salary. The indigent could get in with the flourish of a poem, preferably salacious. They published many broadsheets describing their combined lusts. The public was kept abreast of each perversion, informed on every orgasm, and the faithful leered at the feet of the Master demanding, "What is the Answer?"

Alas, Ginsberg was a Western not an Eastern Master, and as such was preoccupied with his own salvation. He was clocking up time in a personal heaven and probably hadn't even noticed the fast crowd around his ankles. Finding that even nudity was no defense against a Calcutta summer, he left. The government struck. By popular demand the young poets were busted for violating the obscenity laws. Some of the more unforgiving disciples are still waiting for the Master's return.

4

Ginsberg and the Calcutta poets were ahead of their time. The orgies would come but they would come fifteen years later. The gurus would stay, but they would be Indians not Americans. Except for a line of borrowed dialogue. Some popular Indian gurus have taken to answering the increasingly desperate question "What is the Answer?" with a giggle and a soothing "What is the Question?" From the lips of an Indian guru this reply is merely a polite way of finding out where it hurts and when the ache is established, the guru will produce an equally polite, if banal, remedy. The guru does not understand the query, but his international clientele refuse to believe this, so they take his politesse for profundity. Thus, the number of disciples grows and the number of skeptics does not.

In that sense we are more fortunate than those who come to see us. The visitors to India have already suffered from *fatigue de largesse*, which is why they consent to stay with us. From them we have at least heard that all is not well in the lands of plenty, a rumor further reinforced by the spiritual laments being purveyed around the world by the record companies.

Those who visit India on the other hand have not been told often enough or in a popularly comprehensible way that the experience of the East is simply not accessible to the Western mind, except after an almost total reeducation. Yet the common fallacy that sitting for extended periods of time in the lotus position gets you halfway past the wheel of existence is not only not being denied, but is being actively propagated by many ashrams currently in vogue. The gurus have ignored a primary difference between themselves and their disciples.

The Eastern Master when asked "What is the Answer?" has traditionally replied "Who is Asking?" In that lies a central difference between Eastern and Western thought. The East is not concerned with intellectual aggrandizement, so much so that Jung testily called the Eastern mind childish, a mind that didn't even ask questions, but simply perceived them. In a tradition where the question asks itself and the answer replies itself and all that remains is to establish the identity of the asker, clearly the occidental is going to experience serious difficulty in eliciting any information at all, be it spiritual, physical or just the fastest way to get to the next town.

5

Outside a hotel in Benares sits a starving English girl. She has a sketchpad and a quiver of soft lead pencils. She does pointillist studies of India. If you should stop to look over her shoulder she will continue working until she is sure you are interested in her work. Then she will reach shyly into a large mirror-work handbag and take out a sheaf of pictures—exquisite and painstakingly executed studies of temples, burning ghats, Rajput palaces, and Moghul mausoleums—which she will offer for sale.

We got to talking. I acquired a picture and an invitation to come home with her and meet the people she lived with.

"Thanks awfully for taking a drawing. Perhaps we'll have meat tomorrow. I've quite forgotten what meat tastes like."

She gave a little self-conscious laugh.

"I'm afraid I do rather miss meat. You see I was raised on it, great roasts and sausages and game and things."

It was an onerous business getting to where she lived. We had taken a rickshaw, at my insistence, to the riverside bazaar area. She had not looked strong enough to walk in the heat. We had dismounted on the other side of the road to where the shops began. The five square miles of bazaar with its narrow roads and thousands and thousands of shops, the inevitable accretions of a city that had been the heart of the pilgrim's India for several thousand years, would not have been able to accommodate even as small a vehicle as a rickshaw through its winding alleys.

After about forty minutes of walking, dodging past beggars, ignoring the hawkers, avoiding the red spittle of the shopkeepers, the girl beckoned me to cross an overflowing gutter. She led the way up two worn stone steps and into a low doorway. I followed her through a small dark room, past a courtyard crowded with women and children, up a narrow staircase and into a chamber that gave the immediate impression of being a saddlebag. The windows were covered with tattered cloth hangings as was the floor, on which sat three men. Between them was a lighted candle. Two of the men were eating peanuts and the empty shells lay in a circle around them. The third was playing a flute.

They didn't take any notice of the English girl until she brandished her ten-rupee note. The man who was playing the flute looked up, saw the money, placed his instrument carefully on the floor beside him, rose lazily to his feet, and faced her. As if in slow motion he reached up, took the money, and with his other hand gave her a hard open-palmed slap across the face. She reeled backwards and hit the wall, knocking off a hanging, which fell over her like a shroud as she collapsed onto the floor.

"English bitch!" said the man.

I couldn't place his accent, and it was too dark to see him clearly. He might have been Latin, he might have been French. He turned to me with a sneer.

"Her great-grandfather was a viceroy. You people used to lick his shoes. Now you buy her rotten pictures so you can buy her company. Get out! Get out before I throw you out! You're slaves, all of you, filthy beggars . . ."

He put a hand on my shoulder. I pulled away, overcome with irritation at the shoddy charade and this passive girl with her undeniable talent lying whimpering on the floor of a back alley in Benares. I knelt beside the girl and asked her if she was all right. She moaned something.

The two peanut eaters had munched their way undisturbed through the emotional drama above their heads.

"Leave her alone," said one of them through a mouthful of nuts. "The man is telling the truth. About her at any rate. That *is* what she's doing here."

The other peanut eater yawned in agreement and said in a broad Australian accent.

"Yeah, she says she feels guilty about the Opium Wars and her grandfather living in the red sandstone palace in Delhi, and how nobody did anything for the poor. A lot of these Brits are like that. Bleeding hearts. Let him beat her up if that's what she wants. What do you care?"

"Oh God," moaned the girl from the floor.

Ditto, I thought as I went through the doorway.

6

"You should see the Germans," said a Swiss banker turned sadhu. "They are frightening."

"Why frightening?" I asked, interested. "They seem to be a serious lot, and anyway they know more about Hinduism than all the rest of you put together."

The man from Switzerland laughed.

"Know more, hah! But you are right. They have a long tradition with India. Max Mueller and Hitler. Sanskrit and the Swastika. I only say thank the heavens our knowledge is not so deep as theirs."

"What specifically do you find frightening about the Germans in India?"

The Swiss sadhu shook his head in despair.

"What India does to them, what they come here to find. They are not fools like the French, they don't live in slums like the British. No. The Germans go to the mountains, the Himalayas, The Abode of Snow.

"And do you know what they do there? All alone, eighteen thousand feet in the air, next to a frozen glacier, with their books? They try to be Supermen."

The man from Switzerland was getting agitated. Old enmities were taking hold of his imagination.

"It is an extraordinary thing about the Germans. They are like vampires. Waiting, waiting for the twilight of the gods. You know sitting alone in the Himalayas a man can believe the gods are dying. The wind is so shrill. And the Germans wait. To take the place of the gods."

Currently the fastest growing group of Western nationals in India are the Germans, but I was fascinated to know why a Swiss from an Italian canton who was acquainted with the mysteries of international currency should be drawn to the mendicant's trail in India, with its lack of physical, if not spiritual, hygiene.

"It is nothing significant. Just I was tired of dollars, dinars, telephones, telex. For a while I enjoyed this, but a man cannot spend the rest of his life doing a jigsaw puzzle, putting one piece here, another one there, and know he will never see the complete picture."

Picture of what?

"Of myself. Of life. It is here a noisy, dirty silence. So many millions being born, living, dying, without the fuss. This I appreciate. So little fuss. We Swiss are supposed to like order. Well this is order, because in India you are always reminded of the significance and the insignificance of life. In Switzerland it was disordered. In my life I remembered only the significance of banking."

The noisy, dirty silence was broken by the return of the Swiss sadhu's two companions, laden with newly opened coconuts. We tipped the green gourds to our lips gratefully.

"These Canadian guys are paranoid. They think everybody's trying to rip them off," announced one of the companions in exasperation. He turned to me.

"They get here from Toronto or Montreal or wherever with little black notebooks, would you believe? It tells them how much a rickshaw costs, what you should pay for a room, for a coconut. Look at that guy over there, hassling."

In the distance we could see a coconut vendor with his cane stool set in front of him on which was supported a large basket of deep green coconuts. The vendor waved the broad curved knife he used for slicing off the tops of the coconuts. Over him towered a tall blond, vehemently brandishing what appeared to be a diary.

"Do you know what else he's got in that little book?" continued the American. "He's got a figure that tells you what *soap* should cost, for chrissake. Now tell me. What good is that going to do him in India?"

The second companion threw his empty coconut shell on a pile of other green shells, under a tree that cast its stringy shadow on the sand.

"Can't imagine how that book is going to protect him against the real crooks," he said laconically.

"Being Canadian he should know all about that. It's the French he's gotta look out for. They're the real motherstrippers."

And I had thought the French were here for the aesthetics. A shopkeeper had told me that the French always asked for pictures or statues of the God Shiva. This had seemed entirely consistent with the national predilection for style. Who could be closer to Daddy Cool than the Great Ascetic sitting naked on a mountain-top, his only accessory the Third Eye.

The shopkeeper had expanded on his theme.

"When they come to me, the Francesi, I can hear them under the breath chanting *Shiva-o-ham, Shiva-o-ham*. I asked one, 'Brother, do you know what you are saying?' Immediately he gave the reply. 'I am saying I am Shiva.' He knew the meaning of the mantra alright. Can you beat it?"

Another shopkeeper, barely discernible through the strings of beads, mandalas painted on cloth, and bronze butterfat lamps suspended on iron chains, all hanging from the ceiling of his small shop, peered worriedly through his wares at me.

"Sometimes I wonder what will become of these travelers. They cannot be found with Indians. They are like children, you see. It is our gods, not us, who comfort them. They like familiar things like mala beads and incense. They are happy to find so many varieties, sandalwood beads, ivory beads. Rose, jasmine, so many different kinds of incense."

His assistant, a younger man in drainpipe trousers and heavily pomaded coiffure, interjected irritably.

"They are mad. It is alright when they know what to do with these things. Let them go and worship in their church to Mother Mary with the malas and the incense. But they don't want Mother Mary. They want Kali. That shows they are bad charactered."

The older man reconsidered his position.

"No, they are not bad. But I do not think they like beauty anymore. I say, here you are a woman, take the Goddess

Saraswati playing the veena. Or take Tara, like this beautiful piece over here with the turquoise in the forehead. Or at least take Durga Mata riding her tiger. No, they must have Kali, with her garland of skulls, drinking blood.

"I say it will frighten your children. They say Mother Kali shows the strength of the female.

"Tell me, Sister. What do they mean?"

The owner of a bookshop dealing in books relating to mysticism and the occult was more sympathetic.

"At least when they come to my shop they buy books on holy subjects, Yoga, Tantra, *The Gita*, the *Upanishads*. Sometimes I get angry that they do no work when I have a family to feed and prices are so high. But even if they do not work, at least they take the name of God.

"Our Indians, when they come to my shop, they only want to find hot books, about sex and other dirty things.

"You may say these foreigners, they work like donkeys but they think like kings. We Indians, we think like donkeys and we work like kings."

7

It would appear the Eastern Masters knew a thing or two about their own territory. To the question of India, it would seem increasingly legitimate to enquire who wants to know. Someone who's here to get away from there? For the reasons explained by the exhausted filmmaker from Britain?

"The simple answer to the whole movement is that we come here to get unwired. Where else *is* there to go? And here, you're ignored, you're not important at all, so you are forced back on your own resources, not the resources of some huge mammary machine. If you can get used to the indifference, you learn to function again."

India as the new magnet for the new despair. When you're tired of winning come lose with us.

For those who can't take too much indifference, it is enlightening to find that India provides so much that is familiar to the weary traveler.

The Latins, seeing in the saffron-clad sadhu the burgundy robes of the Cardinal. The British, still conscious of the lines of Imperial Vision, retreating from the monuments of conquest to the hair shirts of the slums. The Canadians and the Australians, trapped in their fears of provincialism, following the caravan with an eye on the price tag. The Germans, unable to shed the logic of their scholarship, exorcising Aryan romanticism in the isolated mountain retreats of the Himalayas. And the Grand Optimists, the Americans, trying for the big one—the vault from solitary into nothing. Well, they have the money and we have the time, and few feel shortchanged.

Perhaps the few should look to their point of view.

VI

BEHIND THE
URINE CURTAIN

I

The Indian justly calls his country Rishi Bhoomi, the Land of the Sages. For every seeker there is a sage, destined to teach him true enlightenment. There are even teachers for those skeptics who are of the opinion that the Eyes do not have it, and who prefer to put their miracle where their mouth is. India has proved, more than once, that oral examination is also a path to knowledge.

By following his mouth, an English aristocrat recently discovered an astonishing truth about India. The aristocrat had heard of a guru in a remote village in the depths of Andhra Pradesh, remarkable not only for his enlightenment, but also for his urine, which changed daily into scented rose water. After some hard traveling, the aristocrat rolled up at the correct remote village.

As few outsiders had ever visited this guru, the Englishman was courteously offered a front seat at the morning meditation, when the guru relieved himself of his first miraculous micturition. The aristocrat observed with distant but polite interest that there was a crowd of Indians around the Master's tent, waiting for the guru to complete his ablutions. To the Englishman's surprise, the crowd suddenly turned on him and began bowing him toward the tent. Not wishing to seem cavalier he went to the tent, where the guru's hand opened the curtain and beckoned him to enter.

Inside the tent the Englishman discovered, through the signs and gestures of the Sage, that he was to be privileged to carry the guru's effulgence to the devotees waiting outside. As the warm vessel was placed in his hands, he sniffed the contents.

"It smelled," he later remarked, "like ordinary urine."

Nonetheless, he carried his precious cargo to the crowds outside. The devotees gave him a polite round of applause. Then the cheering got louder. He turned around to see what was going on. The congratulatory din was becoming deafening. When he finally managed to decipher the urgent signals being made by the guru's assistants, the aristocrat grasped that the guru was allowing him, an Englishman—in a gesture of unprecedented magnanimity—to drink the entire contents of the vessel.

"It tasted," observed the aristocrat later, "remarkably like ordinary urine."

2

In India we are keen on defecation. As part of a general concern with purification, which is tied up with recognizing the body as the temple of the soul. Phlegm and feces have no place in a temple. The man who strains toward Nirvana must be sure to void his bowels regularly.

An Indian author has suggested that the homesick Indian remembers most the *cordon insanitaire* that rings our cities. Another Indian author maintains that anyone who, first thing in the morning, cannot face the sight of fifty men ridding themselves of the previous day's indulgences over an open gutter is not strong enough to live in an Indian city. I think the second author has perhaps exaggerated his case, but it is true that one of the invisible blows dealt us by the Industrial Revolution has been the wholly arbitrary construction of private privies.

It is all very well for those who live in a cold climate to insist on Defecation for One, James. For us, that is rather like insisting that people dine alone. It is uncivilized. The communal cleansing is one of the more social moments in the Indian villager's life, and such manners are not singular to the sons of the soil. It is a preoccupation that has influenced many aspects of our culture.

An essential Yoga exercise involves expelling yards and yards of colon, which are then washed in a solution of warm water and salt. For those who ingest no toxins, the early morning micturition is considered a much better pick-me-up than an apple a day.

Unfortunately, our concern with purification does not extend from the body to the street. We often prefer to leave our wastes on the pavement rather than allow them to fester in the flesh. So the odds are that on any given short journey, the inexperienced traveler will have the opportunity of judging for himself whether he is strong enough to look on fifty defecators without blanching.

Like the jogging fanatics, the Indian city dweller is preoc-cupied with keeping his own body, not the civic body, in good running order. He blithely ignores the government signs at every public spot that might tempt the passerby to a quick evacuation, sternly instructing the careless Indian to "Commit No Public Nuisance."

That is the catch in the urban cradle. Being a Public Nuisance. All the aspects of normal living are lumped together under the section titled "Function," and having dealt with that, megalomaniac architects dangle visions of germ-free, glass-domed conurbations before our eyes. Even in India we have begun to forget that men were not made to live under the bell jar. We also long for cities in which the evidence of human occupation is reduced to a bare minimum.

3

A concern with multitude motion is of immediate concern to Indian town planners. No one *teems* like we do.

One Indian architect connected with designing the Twin City of Bombay had of necessity to apply himself to the problem of Mass Rapid Transit Systems. In order to study the problem from an aerial perspective, he positioned himself at an elevated place in front of Bombay's Churchgate, which is the eye of the hurrying and harassed masses of the metropolis. An interstice of overpasses, major roads, and trains, which daily transport three million people to and from work.

The brightest splash of color in that teeming density of humanity is provided by your favorites and mine—the Krishna Consciousness Ensemble. There they are, in the middle of the rush hour, reeling and rocking, Bill Haley bhaktis, bombed out of their minds with the thirty-three thousand repetitions of Hare Krishna, Krishna, Krishna, Hare Rama, Hare, Hare. They have no trains to catch, no mouths to feed, no sick waiting to be attended. They have only to say their beads over and over again, salivating salvation into the dust.

The architect stands on his prominence, suspended high above Churchgate in a construction crane. His multisquared pad balances in front of him. His binoculars are placed on the bridge of his nose, the lenses adjusted, and he has a perfect view of the swirling crowds below. With his binoculars he can distinguish patterns in the mass.

There to the left is a clutch of stiletto-heeled and skirted Goan secretaries, exchanging office gossip in Portuguese. Close behind them are the Kerala clerks in white bush shirts and gray trousers, conversing in Malayam. They are pushed aside by a knot of Maharashtrian fisherwomen who are going home after cleaning the houses of the rich. The fisherwomen are draped in deep-colored saris tied in the Marathi fashion, the fabric pulled tight between their thighs, showing to advantage statuesque buttocks above long brown legs. There go the Gujerati diamond merchants with their loose silk shirts under which are tied money belts holding thousands of rupees' worth of diamonds to their warm bellies. Snaking through the crowds are the lunch delivery men, empty tiffin carriers and dirty dishes balanced precariously on their heads, those geniuses of Bombay who feed a million people of differing diets and preferences every day, without ever writing down an order and without ever making a mistake. A glittering group of Sindhi women gossip their way down the street, fending off the attentions of the jasmine-garland hawkers and the evening-paper boys.

But wait. There in the middle of the rush hour is a widening circle of saffron holding up the proceedings. It has drums, finger cymbals and begging bowls. The architect can hear the beat and the familiar chant Hare Krishna, Hare, Hare filtering up to him through the sound of car horns and horses neighing irritably between the shafts of moth-eaten carriages. The saffron circle seems a gentle, undulating pool of peace in the rushing and shoving going on around it. It sways benignly through the anxious millions teeming home.

The red light turns amber. The dense mass of human beings chatters on, oblivious. All except the Hare Krishnas who are, after all, alumni of Fifth Avenue, Oxford Street, and the Via

Veneto. While the middle eye blinks orange in the sun, they drop the zonked-out act and are across the road like a shot, streaks of saffron lightning. By the time the traffic light turns red, they are already regrouping on the other side of the street, while Bombay's Indians mooch and meander their way across the road, looking for all the world like a population explosion of Hare Krishna heads.

The architect should perhaps be planning a different sort of Twin City, with fewer signals and broader pavements. At the moment he has missed the significance of rhythm on Mass Rapid Transit Systems, the rock and roll methodology.

Otherwise he would have noticed that the streets may be ours, but the lights are theirs.

4

We have a dual attitude toward motion in India, whether of the bowels or of the whole body. The first is done for efficient health, but it is also done for the soul. So too with travel, at some stage the Indian is supposed to travel, not on a specific errand, but for the philosophical education he gets on the journey. Our streets and our stations are thronged with people from a thousand different backgrounds with whom it is practically impossible to avoid conversation. During the conversation you may find that your money has been stolen, or you may find you have been speaking to a sage. Both experiences are considered educational.

As travel becomes more and more efficient, and terminals become indistinguishable and hygienic way stations, the would-be pilgrim is popped like a pellet from one streamlined capsule into another, and his opportunities for conversation and philosophical improvisation are being curtailed.

As a South Indian realist has pointed out:

"When you crash in a train, there you are.
When you crash in a plane, where you are?"

An Indian doctor spoke of the sad case of a crashed American university student who had been brought to him by the ground staff of Pan American World Airways.

The boy, who claimed to be a sadhu in his past life, had dropped a lot of acid shortly before the plane took off from Teheran airport. After about half an hour, when the drug had really begun expanding his mind, he stripped off all his clothes and proceeded to streak up and down the economy section. His first streak was applauded by the younger passengers. By the sixth streak, people were finding his behavior as tedious as the long journey itself. The air hostesses enlisted the aid of the pursers and managed to get the student dressed. Two pursers sat on either side of the boy, holding him down, while the captain radioed ahead to Delhi, requesting medical and religious assistance.

"He kept insisting he was on a nude sadhu trip," said the doctor. "We have a lot of these cases. They are harmless people who want a little attention. But more than that, they want reassurance that they are still human beings from other human beings.

"If you run naked up and down a locked airplane, you will get this reassurance."

5

Elizabeth was shocked to find how India had changed over the last ten years, a change she didn't find the least bit reassuring.

When she had last been in the country she had stayed with Indian friends of her father's. The conversations had been about art and culture, philosophy and family planning. Now she had finished her researches into the Pali scriptures, she was an accredited Doctor of her subject, and had agreed—for a handsome sum—to return to India after a decade to take a select group of art lovers around the temples of India.

The tour of India's great temples brought Elizabeth and her group eventually to Khajuraho, a collection of temples sculpted from top to bottom with erotic figures. After making a short explanatory lecture on the significance of eroticism on Indian mysticism, Elizabeth allowed her group to wander around the temples at their own leisure. She herself took the opportunity to enjoy again her favorite sculpture, the one with the elephant, the king, the three courtesans, and the two assistants of indeterminate sex.

Elizabeth stolidly ignored the banter of the bumptious guide behind her, a young man with greasy locks falling suggestively into hooded black eyes.

"You like?" he enquired breathily, as she contemplated the sculpture.

"Yes, thank you," said Elizabeth, turning to the next monument of erotica. The guide stepped a little closer.

"You like?"

Elizabeth pretended she hadn't heard, and moved from one erotic frieze to another.

"You like? You like?" came the persistent enquiry from her rear.

Elizabeth firmly rounded the corner to find her stiff upper lip confronted by the even stiffer features of an entire wall devoted to the pleasures of Onan.

"You like?" shouted the eager voice behind her. Elizabeth could take no more. She turned furiously on her tormentor,

"Why can't you piss off! I don't have to tell you what I like!"

The young man only understood her last words. A smile of pure pleasure spread across his face. His brilliantined hair gleamed like black gold in the sun.

"You like!" he said accusingly, and Elizabeth found herself looking at an Indian temple guide in the full frontal exposure. She took to her heels. The young man shouted after her,

"Why? Why? You like! Even I like! Come back! Enjoy!"

6

Few Indians believe anymore that the motives of the foreign tourists who come to see the great erotic temples are cultural and not prurient. Their suspicions have been confirmed by the foreign communities that spring up around these temples during the tourist season, housed under tattered saris suspended on bamboo poles, communities whose members are prepared to re-enact some of the temple motifs for paying customers. The locals now shrug them off as just another scam that keeps the tourist currency in circulation.

The truth is, so long as it doesn't affect their sons and daughters, Indians are not overly concerned with the carryings-on of the international fast set. It is other foreigners, like Elizabeth, who find their sense of inviolability wounded. The educated tourist is well aware of the dangers of breaking down those invisible and visible barriers that sustain spiritual distinction. Not for nothing were the Englishmen who manned the Indian Civil Service instructed to wear black tie for dinner every evening of their stay in India, regardless of the surroundings. Town, village or temple, the civilized man emphasized the difference before someone lapsed into familiarity.

The itinerant travelers who sweep through India today don't dress for dinner, and are treated by the natives with a corresponding informality.

7

The moment when *pudeur* lost to pornography can perhaps be dated to the time when the hippies first discovered the bone-white beaches of Goa.

In those days the hippies were freaking out to Nature in her most primitive and romantic guise. Goa not only had beaches and Rousseauesque jungles, but it even had a monkey as one of its major deities, the God Hanuman. The hippies didn't know that Hanuman is worshiped as the Custodian of Honor. What they saw was whole temples given over to monkeys, swinging up and down from the vines of banyan trees, chattering in the temple forecourts, snatching food out of the hands of worshiping devotees. The Goans didn't know the hippies hadn't come for a carnival. What they saw were musicians, with flutes and guitars, singing in the moonlight. Everyone showed up at Calingute Beach for a Happening. Eventually it happened.

Calingute Beach was also used as a shortcut by little Indian Christian schoolgirls, led by novitiates hiding behind cowls and veils, to get to the convent on the other side of the beach for their daily catechism lessons. Imagine the shock of the tiny demoiselles, under the basilisk gaze of their stern duennas, when they came upon the following scene of merriment: hundreds of naked bodies, of every hue and national origin, coupling in the sand. In the middle of the alfresco sensuality cavorted monkeys, pinching a thigh here, the nape of a neck there.

The nuns hurried their wards past the landscape of sin. They had taught generations of young Christian ladies that men have animal passions, but they had never had the misfortune of proving it.

The nuns described the scene to the Bishop. The Bishop consulted the tonwspeople, and was informed by the Hindu fishermen that the hippies were adopting baby monkeys from the temple precincts and suckling them. There was also a strong rumor that a few avant-garde hippies were actually mating with the monkeys, though no one in town had actually witnessed this with his own eyes. It was decided that steps must be taken to bring perversion to a halt.

Parents, priests, and publicans joined in the battle. Giggling schoolgirls stenciled onto banners such slogans as "Ban Breast-feeding of Monkeys on the Beach," and "Lot's Wife Go Home." Bearing these severe admonishments the town took a procession to the Municipal Corporation, who were discovered to be too embarrassed to go down to the beach and personally stop the orgies.

Political torpor was no match for such wayward behavior, so the authorities took the line of least resistance. The hippies weren't actually harming anyone. Perhaps it would be best if the schoolgirls took a longer route to the convent, bypassing the spectacle of the beach.

Thus the Corporation avoided creating a national scandal, and succeeded in creating a national sport. Goa now has two unique attractions. The beach, for the tourist who wants cheap thrills, and the Cathedral, for the tourist of a religious bent.

8

The flowering of Portuguese imperialism in Goa is fittingly enshrined in the great Bom Jesus Cathedral, with its gold leaf, vaulting arches, and warrens of chapels. The High Altar is a tower of ascending saints, hands outstretched to a cloud on which floats the Madonna, an infant Jesus in her arms.

The Cathedral can in splendor challenge anything built by Cortez to dwarf the pyramids of Montezuma and establish the supremacy of Mother Church, but in the rich light filtering through the windows, one can see the hand of the Indian artisans who embellished the edifice. Wall upon wall of the Cathedral is sculpted with saints displaying huge, ripe breasts and lyre-shaped thighs. Doe-like eyes slant out invitingly to the faithful, over lips puckered in promise of Heaven.

The Bom Jesus Cathedral, like all significant places of worship in India, is a repository of the miraculous. It is the resting place of the mortal remains of the great Jesuit saint and missionary Francis Xavier. The saint's body, miraculously intact since the sixteenth century, used to be exposed every year on his birthday, for millions of faithful who congregated from all over the world to light candles, attend High Mass, and pray for further miracles. Great lines of people would kneel in front of the altar where St. Francis Xavier reclined, and open their mouths to receive the holy wafer.

About eighty years ago, a portly doubter queued up with the rest of the faithful to file past the coffin. At the *moment critique* she was assailed with doubt that the body was real. So she knelt down, bent over, and bit off St. Francis Xavier's big toe. The body turned out to be flesh and blood after all, and she was stuck with the evidence in her mouth. She left the Cathedral and went home as fast as her stocky legs could carry her. But she wasn't fast enough. A trail of miraculous blood pursued her. When she looked over her shoulder and saw that she was being tracked down by the saint's blood, she spat out the toe and begged forgiveness for her profanity.

As a result, the wondrous hulk is now shown only once every twelve years, and even then it is guarded against doubt by a fence. If you should happen to hit Goa on the wrong year, a monstrance is produced from the holy of holies chapel, a huge brocade banner framed in twenty-four carat gold, borne aloft by proud papists. There is a center to the mandala. The brocade and the gold are just the mounting for St. Francis Xavier's toe.

If you wish, the priests will lower the banner, and allow you to kiss the glass that covers the miraculous metatarsal. Some would advise against it.

Conventional wisdom has it that a kiss is just a kiss. But in India, who knows? Whether you are an English aristocrat inspired by Hindu faith, or just an Indian housewife torn by Christian doubts, in the Land of the Sages it is probably politic to keep the mouth free of foreign objects.

In order to avoid the humiliating alternatives of swallowing everything you hear. Or having to spit out the obvious.

VII

.

FORKED TONGUES

1

It had been one of those dull late nights. We sat in a high-ceilinged room in Calcutta's fashionable Alipore, watching the fans go round and round, desultorily discussing which horse would win the Invitation Cup. Starched servants served chilled vodka cut with green chilies to an assortment of jockeys, industrialists and princes. Occasionally a large, velvety bat would dive-bomb the jasmine bushes beyond the balcony and all the ladies would scream. I sat with my drunk and languid escort in a paralysis of ennui.

"Would you like some charas?" asked a stranger.

It was four o'clock in the morning. A woman was weeping with emotion as Roberta Flack keened, "Strumming my life with his fingers . . . killing me softly with his song."

Charas seemed like a good metaphor for action. I nudged my escort awake.

"He has some dope. Shall we?"

Some nights you can safely ignore the manners. Without farewells we navigated our way down the marble staircase. In one of the cars parked outside my escort located his chauffeur, shook him awake and told the stranger to direct. Then he passed out.

The silence of the journey was punctuated by arguments between the stranger and the chauffeur. They must have reached an amicable agreement because we rolled up at the gates of the right house.

The stranger beckoned us in. My escort straightened his dinner jacket, instructed the chauffeur to wait, and followed us. The stranger lived in a large dark house with servants sleeping across the doorways to every room. We silently stepped over their immobile forms, making our way in total darkness from hallway to drawing room to dining room to study, until we finally arrived in the stranger's bedroom.

"This is my sister's house," said the stranger by way of explanation, and switched on the lights.

My escort took in the arrangements, noted a cot in the corner, its lumps covered by a blanket, staggered toward it, lay down, and passed out.

The stranger opened a large Victorian cupboard, pulled out a plastic bag, and began his preparations.

"Have you got a light?" asked the stranger.

"No I'm sorry," I replied.

The stranger looked at my escort.

"He doesn't smoke," I said.

In one corner of the room was an altar. The wall was covered with colorful portraits of Indian gods painted on glass. Below the portraits was a large silver tray holding bronze statues. Krishna rolling his pat of butter. Devi, sitting cross-legged and bare breasted on a lotus. Ganesh standing with one hip thrust out, smiling behind his elephant's trunk. In front of the bronzes was a clay lamp filled with oil. Its wick burned brightly. The stranger held a lump of hash over the flame. It crumbled between his fingers. Then he filled a chillum, which we smoked in companionable silence. After two more chillums he volunteered the information that he was a tax specialist.

"Do you believe in the gods?" I asked, pointing at the altar.

"Sure," he said.

"Don't you think it's disrespectful to heat dope at the sacrificial flame?"

"Nope."

My escort got up and indicated that it was time to leave. The lumps on the cot vacated by my escort moved. The blanket fell aside and a fully uniformed guard sprang off the cot and saluted sheepishly.

The stranger was looking thoughtfully into the flame in front of the altar.

"God's cool," he stated with simple finality.

"How true," said my escort and we left.

2

In New York on a stifling June afternoon, I am with some friends in a large American car trying to get to Central Park. At Sixty-first and Fifth someone is pulling away from the curb. Someone else is trying to back into the same space, effectively preventing the first vehicle from departing. We are ideally placed to steal the parking space should either car succeed in moving at all.

A passenger in our car wakes from his torpor to shout,

"That guy is moving out. Sneak in fast!"

We are being driven by a benign American Semite, who is now a Sufi. He takes no notice of the advice being tendered from the back seat. Someone thinks he hasn't noticed and pounds him on the shoulder.

"Look! That guy's leaving. Grab his spot!"

Our Sufi friend looks into the rear view mirror at his back seat adviser. In a soft and patient voice he explains,

"Fuck, man, I can't do that. Karmically speaking, it's bad design."

You keep hearing the wrong song in the wrong place.

3

There was a time when people knew who they were and the occasional miscomprehensions were funny. In a Paris striptease parlor the non-English-speaking disc jockey used to play St. James' Infirmary as background music for the saloon's hottest stripper, a black girl from Martinique. While the speakers blared

She was laid out on a long white table
So cold, so dead, so fair . . .

the lady from Martinique, happily oblivious of the meaning of the dirge, would do her bumps and grinds to wild cheers from an international audience and an occasional double take from those who spoke English.

But that was way back in the Fifties when it was still possible to identify those who spoke English. In India anyway. Those of us who spoke it at all spoke in well-rounded sentences with more than a hint of Macaulayan grammar. True, the great Indian patriot Sarojini Naidi had publicly called Mahatma Gandhi her "little Mickey Mouse" forty years ago, but Dell Comics had not yet devastated our minds leaving us easy prey to the fractured prose of America.

By the Sixties, modulation had given way to acceleration. The explosive shorthand of America seemed infinitely preferable to the dilatory obliqueness of England.

By the Seventies, elderly Indian politicians who had never heard of the Mafia were demonstrating at Delhi Airport with placards reading "Kissinger of Death Go Home!" and a national Indian newspaper, with perfect linguistic confidence, carried the headline "Fag Hag Crooner."

On the other side of the planet the world's fastest speech looked for new words for slowing down. For twenty years we had burrowed in their vocabulary, now they scavenged in ours. Together with their own "laid backs" and "mellowed outs" went our Karmas, Sadhanas, Nirvanas, Tantras, and Sanyas.

With language as with goods you take what you need. The British took from us jodhpurs and bungalows, riding breeches and colonial cottages, words for a more settled times. We had taken the idiom of modern America because it seemed to have no discernible provenance, a spontaneous verbalism that embraced the immediate as well as the immediate future. But now that America has taken our most complicated philosophical concepts as part of its everyday slang, things are getting sticky. Whose interpretations should be accepted as final authority—the Sanskrit scholar's or the street hustler's?

It is ironic that we should have become so giddy in the presence of energy when energy, power, *Shakti*—in its demonic and constructive forms—has been the subject of philosophical consideration in India for roughly four thousand years. It is also ironic that of all the terms from Hindu philosophy that have captured the American imagination, none has greater currency than karma—and that, in the last fifteen years, for a generation disenchanted by war.

In the most popular dialogue on karma, read by all devout Hindus in *The Bhagavad Gita*, Arjuna is given no option on the specific issue of war. Arjuna begs his charioteer, the god Krishna, for a reason why he should go into battle against his teachers, members of his family and friends:

"Should not we whose eyes are open turn away from so great a crime? If you deem the path of understanding more excellent than the path of action, O Krishna, why do you urge me to do this savage deed?"

The god Krishna gives Arjuna no sops against desolation, not even the easy answers of a martial or proselytizing culture—a just war, a pious war, a war of liberation. Krishna answers Arjuna's plea with the implacable words:

"Because you are bound to act. Only action will save you from the bondage of action."

That's karma. Or what it used to be. That's also what the god Krishna used to be. A Blue Meanie.

Not any longer. Karma is now *felt* as a sort of vibration and Krishna is a doe-eyed pinup. As options proliferate all over the globe, the ability to understand the nature of necessity appears to be diminishing and bondage means something else again. So the terminology has accommodated itself to the needs of those who use it.

"I can't visit London anymore. The Karma there is too heavy for me," says the Iranian hairdresser.

"I crashed my car last night. I have bad Karma," says the Mexican student.

"That dude's dangerous. He has heav-y Karma," says the Harlem drug dealer.

"Craps—it's a low Karma game," explains the American gambler's girlfriend.

"My daughter is called Rani," says the German mother. "The night she was born in Goa my friend and his lady had a daughter in Los Angelos and they called her Rani. We have such *close* karma."

Coincidence, chance, *déjà vu*, anything goes as karma. It is fortunate that the elaborate Hindu pantheon is really a dance routine only meant to hold your interest until you get over being stagestruck, and does not culminate in a Zeus or a Jehovah waiting to let you have it with a lightning rod for the crime of blasphemy; because if ever the karma was right for the gods to warn Here comes the Judge, it would seem to be now.

4

While we shake, rattle and roll, and the visitor remains preoccupied with vibrating, a lot of energy is wasted in ignoring the central paradoxes. The principle of karma is a bad choice for narcosis. The Karmic Law would seem to suggest that there is no heaven, only a series of life sentences, and that salvation occurs not in an after-life paradise but with a successful death.

For us eternal life is death—not in the bosom of Jesus—but just death, no more being born again to endure life again to die again. Yet people come in ever-increasing numbers to India to be born again with the conviction that in their rebirth they will relearn to live. At the heart of all our celebrations, which are still lively and colorful, is the realization that we are at a wake. But the tourists we draw because of that color and that liveliness appear to think that they are at a christening.

We hope that progress, enquiry, as defined by the West, may somehow free us from the constraints of having to be endlessly cross-eyed, having to see the finite and the infinite in everything.

But it is precisely this business of being cross-eyed that so attracts the outsider. Only he finds the spiritual squint attractive because he is doing the squinting. It is his perception of himself as the philosopher and not as the victim of the philosophy that permits him to be so enthusiastic, an enthusiasm that stems from the hiatus between the Western emphasis on conquest and the Eastern emphasis on endurance.

It is unlikely that either the Occidental or the Easterner has the stamina to survive this exchange of views, yet both insist on trying and both use irrelevant language to camouflage the contradictions. It is unlikely that the Easterner is good enough to look closely at the parts and not lose his ability to view the whole, so he calls what fascinates him in the West economic necessity, technology, historical imperative. It is unlikely that the Occidental can see the whole and not lose his highly developed capacity and compulsion to question, so he calls what fascinates him in the East the transcendence of economics and technology, the antidote to history. Both cloak the enemies of their strengths in new terminology and hope to render them harmless.

The Westerner is finding the dialectics of history less fascinating than the endless opportunities for narcissism provided by the Wisdom of the East. Except that the prime concern of the Wisdom of the East is the annihilation of narcissism.

And so on ad nauseam.

5

There is a popular rumor that India can turn nausea into serenity.

Perhaps a natural successor to the rumor abroad during the aftermath of the Second World War about the Catholic Church.

Then there was a mushrooming of Trappist monasteries, with people turning their nausea into contemplative silence. Now there is a stampede to India with people turning their nausea into a dysentery of inscrutable terminology. India has been only too happy to join in the stampede.

The Indian national airline, which handles all air traffic inside the country, had an advertisement used for publication in foreign magazines boasting of an airfare that provided "Nirvana for $100 a Day."

A guru who has an ashram in Western India with a large number of foreign followers, confided to a correspondent from *Time* magazine,

"My followers have no time. So I give them instant salvation. I turn them into neo-sanyasis."

A sanyasi in India is halfway to being a saint, a man who has renounced the world to seek the truth, a renunciation that is social as well as physical. His vows are not significantly different from those who join monasteries in the West—dedication to poverty, chastity, and if the sanyasi has a teacher, obedience. But the simple-minded Hindu, when he comes upon two light-skinned strangers in the bazaar, sharing a chillum of hashish while they fondle each other, is apt to think that the strangers are wearing the sadhu's orange robes of renunciation as an act of aggressive mockery. The simple Hindu, unlike the sophisticated guru, has not incorporated such concepts as "neo" or "instant" into either his daily or his religious vocabulary.

It would appear that when East meets West all you get is the neo-Sanyasi, the instant Nirvana. Coming at the problem from separate directions, both parties have chanced upon the same conclusion, namely, that the most effective weapon against irony is to reduce everything to the banal. You have the Karma, we'll take the Coca-Cola, a metaphysical soft drink for a physical one.

One guru wrote a long piece in an Indian magazine explaining his views on the Apocalypse, which was in its way a perfect example of what happens when great cultures meet. He wrote,

"Everything is perfect. But also the Third World War is coming! That is going to be perfect too! It will kill *utterly*."

A mind reared on relativity can't help overheating at the excitement of the absolutely absolute.

"You are sitting on a volcano. Never before was it so dangerous. And you think, What are you doing here, meditating? What else can you do?

"Meditate while the time is still there! If the volcano erupts and you die meditating you will know the taste of the deathless!"

This guru enjoys the reputation of being the thinking man's guru.

For the less intellectually demanding, there are gurus like the eternal teenager Guru Maharaj Ji, who once hired Houston Astrodome in order to spread his teachings. Maharaj Ji sat on an elaborate throne spotlighted from every direction. Behind him rose the huge stadium scoreboard, which carried in blazing lights the encouraging Eastern message: ENJOY ENJOY ENJOY.

Yet another guru bolsters the faith of his followers in an indoor football stadium in Delhi by promising proof of the existence of God. The man has been seen to perform miracles by thousands, so people are predisposed to grant him supernatural insight into logic and semantics. The masses wait with bated breath.

The guru informs them, through the medium of a simultaneous translator, that God exists because if you look in the Oxford English Dictionary under the letter G, you will eventually find the word God. Triumphantly the guru raises his short arms in benediction to the nonplussed but believing audience, sitting in tightly fitted rows on the vast field where six hours ago sweating athletes raced up and down in pursuit of a ball, and announces,

"It is in the Dictionary. Let those who doubt the existence of the divine look for proof in the Dictionary. How could what does not exist, then exist in the Dictionary?"

The guru's following over the last few years has become so extensive that he now has to give benediction from a helicopter. On his birthday hymns of praise burst from the throats of a million earthbound believers, addressed to the little orange speck of certainty waving down at them from a flying machine in the sky.

To some gurus, current dictionaries are inadequate to take on such weighty issues as mysticism, let alone provide proof of the existence of God. Among these gurus is the man who briefly shared with Buddy Holly the distinction of being teacher to the Beatles—the Maharishi.

6

The Maharishi stopped off in Delhi last winter to hold audience for four days and four nights in a large suite in the city's most expensive hotel. He received in his bedroom, clad simply in a lungi of the finest silk, his bare shoulders covered with a white silk shawl. The several hundred applicants were shown into the drawing room, the dining room, and the secretary's chambers—all parts of the suite—to wait until their names were called for a private audience.

To help them while away the time profitably, the supplicants were given large armfuls of expensively printed literature describing the guru's latest enthusiasm, a "Blueprint for World

Government," as well as literature describing the success of his old enthusiasms, such as defense strategy and military might, projections on how far the world's self-destructive tendencies had been contained by the good vibrations emanating from him and his followers, and of course, the great and necessary power of Transcendental Meditation.

The devotees had pinned posters on the walls of the waiting rooms. On first sight these colorful, well-designed pictures seemed to be tourist advertisements. But that was only because of the gloss and the scenery. On closer inspection they turned out to be spectacular examples of the success of the Maharishi's teachings. The illustrations, which covered every inch of available wall space, showed the Maharishi's students at his ashram in Switzerland in various degrees of levitation. The expressions of those who had left the ground conveyed heady excitement, complete disbelief, pure bliss, and in only one case, as the subject peered nervously over his crossed legs, vertigo.

I shared my audience time with the Maharishi with four other people: two Italian countesses, an Indian nuclear physicist, and an English scientist doing biochemical research. The Italian women engaged the Maharishi's attention first. One of them had been in India several months, the other and older woman, only ten days. The younger woman did the talking for both of them. She explained that she had been initiated into Transcendental Meditation at one of the centers outside Rome, and her friend had come to India to be initiated into meditation by the Maharishi himself.

"But, Swami," ended the Countess, "my mantra is not working anymore."

"Oh dear," said the Maharishi, and continued to smile. "Then we must give you another. Use the new mantra for four days, then let him know," and he pointed to a man kneeling piously in the dark corner, "whether it is working. I won't be here. I must fly back to Switzerland tomorrow. My work requires me there."

The Countess seemed completely consoled. I wondered at the credulity of her friend, who had just witnessed that the efficacy of the mantra was not total, nor did meditation produce transcendence yet she was determined to have one.

The second Countess was at least sixty years old, lived a stone's throw from the Vatican, and was a practicing Catholic. She was also not a fool. But she believed so totally in the power of this incomprehensible word from another religion and in an unknown language that she had paid the airfare from Rome to Delhi for the express purpose of wresting it from the Maharishi's obliging lips.

Later, just before she went into insulin shock owing to the unforeseen delays in the Maharishi's dining room, which had adversely affected her blood sugar count, she explained,

"This mantra, it is only for me. It is the connection between myself and the peace. My son is dead. My daughters are married. I am old and lonely. I have need of the Peace."

Back at the Vatican they were offering the "peace that passeth understanding." But it wasn't enough for the Countess. What she wanted was Shanti with a name tag. A specific, not a general reprieve. And if it meant spending the next few years following the Maharishi around the globe exchanging new mantras for old ones, then that was the price of an individual fitting.

Haute couture always costs more than *prêt-à-porter*.

The Maharishi, having dispensed with the demands of the Italian women, turned eagerly to the Indian nuclear physicist and the English biochemist. They were to be participants in his newest inspiration, a World Conference on Chemistry, Physics, and Transcendental Meditation. The year before he had been interested in armies and armaments, and somehow convinced the military Establishment to espouse the cause of Transcendental Meditation. The military Establishment had recognized in the Maharishi's teachings a key that could turn men from cannon fodder into samurai. Fresh from such triumph, the Maharishi had now turned his celestial energy to the problem of harnessing the potential of science.

The two scientists watched his preparatory giggles with clinical detachment, trying to hide their dismay from each other and from the guru's sharp eye. Rationalism lost out to curiosity and they decided to stay.

"You see, my friends," said the guru, "science is only beginning to catch up with the knowledge that we Indian mystics have had through the ages. Once you have scientific words for what we know and teach, then you will accept the truth of what we say. Until then you will consider us fools. What it amounts to is that you wish to make up your own mantras."

The Maharishi giggled wickedly at the scientists.

"For instance, anyone who is seriously interested and will not disturb, is welcome to come to Switzerland and see for themselves whether my students can levitate. But so many who come, go away and say they were hypnotized."

The Maharishi keeled over sideways in a fit of high-pitched laughter.

"They say they were hypnotized because they consider themselves intelligent and *know* there is no such thing as levitation. So they say it is magic. But intelligent people are not supposed to believe in magic either, are they, my scientific friends?"

The scientists were looking at the guru with greater interest. "After all," continued the Maharishi, "what is there in levitation? In meditation we teach people to go below the layer of the conscious mind to their center. The center is where the energy is totally concentrated. So what is there magical in all this? We teach our students that by concentration through meditation they can create an impenetrable field of energy between the ground and their bodies. The greater the field of energy, the higher the meditating man can rise. It is simple *Q.E.D.*"

By now the Maharishi had succeeded in capturing the full attention of the scientists. He was using their language.

"Am I not telling the truth?" asked the Master, warming to his task. "For thousands of years we have been searching for the essence, the particle. The particle, no, gentlemen? How you all thought when you found the atom that you had the answer. Then what do you find? Electrons, neutrons, and now what? The particle. We are not such fools as you think. If you had asked us we would have told you . . . and I am warning you now . . . you still do not have the answer. You are getting there, but it will take you another forty or fifty years.

"Then perhaps you will understand that even your particle is not what you think. Because, scientists, your particle is only shakti. It is only energy. Where is buddhi? Where is the intelligence of life?"

The Maharishi reached out and gave a marigold from the garlands lying at his feet to the biochemist. The Englishman blushed and attempted an awkward namaste. Then the Maharishi emphatically pulled a red rose out of the garlands and handed it to the nuclear physicist. The Indian accepted the flower nervously. It was clear from the expression on his face that he suspected that the gift might drain some of the power he had acquired from a lifetime of pursuing the rational. The Maharishi's enthusiasm for his new project covered the self-consciousness of both scientists.

"Come, gentlemen. Let us join hands. It is Kalyug. The Age of Darkness. We have no time to wait thirty or forty years for scientists to find the right words. The moral issues are already clear.

"Look around you. See what it is possible to achieve. Look how the world is thirsty. People everywhere are crying 'Show us the Way!' Is it not funny that they are asking this during Kalyug, the most immoral of eras?" The Maharishi giggled in delight.

"But we can do it together, that is what is really funny. And only in these times when your knowledge is so close to our wisdom.

"In six months I am inviting all the top scientists of the world to a conference to discuss. I hope you will join us. My secretary will give you the details."

The guru then blessed the scientists and they got up to leave. As they opened the door leading into the crowded sitting room, the Maharishi shouted after them, "Gentlemen, remember my words. It is time to ring the bell for EUREKA!"

7

Such impressive throwaway lines reduce a lot of the permanent residents in Eastern retreats to speechlessness. It is their misfortune that while their tongues are silenced by the incoherence, their ambitions are not. The desire to taste the deathless is not easily quenched.

I once shared a house with several people who could not find accommodation in an overcrowded ashram. Among them was a Scandinavian girl who had been through many forms of meditation in her three-year stay in India. She had left language, reliving her past and even primal screaming, far behind her.

What she did now, all day and most of the night, was sit on a rocking chair in front of a small wooden table where joss sticks burned before two silver frames, which held a photograph of her guru and a crudely drawn crayon portrait of herself. She stared at these pictures for hours on end and hummed. There was no melody in her humming. Just the same two notes, over and over again.

An irate Indian photographer was also staying at the house. He had recently returned from the Indo-Tibetan border where he had been photographing Buddhist monasteries. In the mountains he had found that the Buddhist monks were humming since friendly tourists and government bureaucrats had pressed tape recorders and transistor radios upon them. Now here, on the hot Deccan plains, was this girl's steady drone following him around the house.

On the third night, after having listened to the Scandinavian girl hum, for what by his calculations was a period of seventy-three hours, the photographer turned to me and whispered savagely,

"If she doesn't stop at midnight I'm going to ask her what's happening, whatever damage it does her immortal soul. I shall put it to her plainly. I am going to say,

'Why are you still *humming*, woman? Don't you know the words?'"

VIII

VOX POX

I

Several years ago, in a Manhattan jazz club, a shy little man in white homespun shirt and pajamas sent a written request to play with the band. The leader of the jazz band read the note and asked the waiter who had sent it. The waiter pointed to an Indian gentleman at a back table. The leader peered through his reflecting dark glasses and beckoned the stranger to come onstage.

The Indian left the table with some difficulty and bumped his way through the curious audience to the small raised stage. His progress was hampered by a pair of Indian drums he was carrying in his left hand.

"What's that?" asked the leader.

"My drums, sir," answered the Indian. "If I am to play with you I must use my own instrument, the tabla."

"Oh yeah, the drums. So you want to play with us," said the jazz musician. "Well, whaddya want to play?"

"Myself, I would like to play in Teen Taal," said the Indian diffidently. "That is your three times."

He explained his plan. "You please play in this basic rhythm And I shall accompany on the tabla with seventy-two beats from my right hand and twenty-four beats from my left hand, and then increasing with the improvising."

The Indian cleared a space on the ground for himself, untied his shoelaces, took off his shoes and placed them neatly under the piano. From the cloth bag on his shoulder he extracted a small silver hammer. With this he began to hit the pegs on the sides of his instruments.

The jazz musician grinned at the crowd, leaned over and asked the little man, "Seventy-two and twenty-four, huh? Okay. Say, what you doing down there with that hammer?"

"I am tuning, sir. May you ask the piano player to tell which key you will prefer?"

The leader turned to the pianist with a shrug and said, "This guy's crazy. Give him a G and get him out of here."

The piano player, with exaggerated formality, played a G octave. The Indian nodded and hit the pegs on his drums harder.

"Yes. Pa. Pa. Pa," he sang to his drums, using the Indian word for the G note.

"I think he wants to play 'My Heart Belongs to Daddy,'" said the pianist, winking broadly at the appreciative audience.

The leader sat down behind his own drums in resignation, nodded to the vibraphone player, picked up his sticks, and shouted, "Well all *right!*" and the jazz band broke into a fast blues.

The little Indian beamed with pleasure. His hands began to move over his drums. A hollow bass emerged from his left drum, his other hand was almost invisible as it moved over the right drum. After a few minutes the leader put his sticks down and shook his head in disbelief. Then the bass player stopped to listen. Now it was a duet between the piano and the Indian. The piano would play a melody and the tabla would reproduce it in double time, then in triple time. The leader came in again using his drums to create a solid three-beat backing to the Indian's intricate rhythms. The Indian and the piano player were laughing with pleasure. The pianist jumped up and down as he played his instrument, the Indian shook his head in an ecstasy of invention. On each downbeat he would crane his neck around to look at the leader and then bring his head down sharply so they could both hit their drums in unison. The pace got faster and faster, the crowd was on its feet, cheering and whistling.

When the performance came to an end the jazz musician took off his dark glasses and wiped his face.

"Who are you, man? Where did you learn to play like that?"

"That was most enjoyable, sir," said the little man. "I learned my art in Benares. UNESCO has brought me here to make it popular to the West. I hope it gave pleasure."

The Indian collected his shoes, bowed in deep namaste to each member of the band, picked up his hammer and drums and left. He didn't know that he had just played with the most famous jazz drummer in the West. The jazz musician didn't know he had accompanied India's most distinguished tabla maestro. But they'd had a beat encounter.

2

Bombay recently hosted a week-long jazz festival aptly titled Indo-Jazz Yatra. For Jazz, read foreign. Yatra means journey. The Indian Foreign Journey.

The Journey took place in an open-air auditorium in the heart of urban Bombay. The auditorium was ringed on three sides by the gray-stone neo-Gothic buildings of St. Xavier's College, constructed at a time when dreaming spires and higher learning were more or less synonymous in the British mind. India was represented by the flora and fauna. Large banyan trees broke through the cultural pretensions, leaves obscured by tattered kites, roots overrun by Bombay rats scurrying in and out of the Event.

The people who had conceived the idea were mostly Parsis and Gujeratis: by day, captains of industry, big wheels on the stock exchange and the textile market. Middle-aged, powerful and erudite men, they had succeeded in transporting sixteen jazz bands from all over the world to play Bombay for free, and they now spent their evenings arguing the merits of a Polish tenor sax against those of a Japanese bass guitar, while the Poles and the Japanese spent their mornings discussing the merits of the raga form.

The jazz commenced every morning at seven o'clock and continued until about three in the morning. The male jazz buffs had made no toilet arrangements for the women. In a nightly audience of two thousand people, there were inevitably a few women with weak bladders, their situation made more poignant by the open gutter that ran down the entire left flank of the auditorium. Some oblivion from the smell of urine was provided by the waves of hashish, which rolled over the audience, emanating from the college students in the back rows. Behind these rows, to the left of the men's lavatory, five separate kitchens were in active operation, cooking and selling vegetarian and nonvegetarian food. As the night drew on, occasionally an attic window lit up in St. Xavier's College, revealing a white-robed Jesuit standing motionless four floors above the frenzy below.

One man had been saddled with the responsibility of holding the anarchic instincts of the Indians in check. It was his function to remind the people queuing for food, the ladies bewailing the absence of toilets, the junkies in the back row, the bazaar wallahs behind them, the crush of foreigners at the gates trying to get in free, the cooks and the cops, that they were here to listen to the music. He was, so the cognoscenti assured us, *the*

Voice of America. The guru who had led them by high-frequency wave from a distance of several thousand miles through the many intricacies of jazz, interpreting the riffs, decoding the scat. His disembodied voice had been so seductive that it had turned many of those who might have otherwise patronized the sitar and the mridangam, to the patronage of the music of black America. These patrons kept alive numerous Indian jazz combos whose only dream was to play with the American greats.

Thirty years after he had set the ball rolling, here was the Voice of America in person, an oldish gray-haired man in cotton trousers and a button-down shirt, perspiring in the humidity, peering past the quartz iodine bulbs of an Eastern European television crew to where his alumni sat, indistinct in the warm Bombay night.

Beneath him a chemically inspired Canadian danced every night from the opening chords to the moment the instruments were packed away.

The Canadian wore a loose orange shirt open to the waist, over flowing maroon pantaloons. Around his neck was a selection of pendants, malas and other signifying jewelry. In the focused television lights, against the banks of black amplifiers, the colorful gyrating figure lost in complicated modes of physical expression looked like a temple dancer, trying to ground the gods with footwork.

The stage was protected from the marathon dancer by the rigid figure of a Bombay policeman, a smile of embarrassment frozen on his face.

That frozen smile reappeared on the faces of the Indian audience at the morning sessions of the Indo-Jazz Yatra when the Indian maestros performed. The Indians were following the philosophy of the musicians, for which the maestros had undergone such arduous training to win the title of Ustad, Pandit, Teacher. But the festival had created an atmosphere of sufficient general confusion that visiting jazz musicians mistook it for a jam session, leaping onstage to interrupt the Bhairav, the raga of rebirth with the muted sobbings of a trombone. Or as happened at one morning session, with the whip sounds of a large steel saw.

The smile never thawed to anger. Fortunately, one of the bonuses provided by mass communication is that anything goes. If it can be heard, it can be relayed. And if it doesn't make sense, the machine needs servicing.

The art of dialing has replaced the art of dialogue. When the person on the other end of the receiver doesn't understand the conversation, then drop the hard part, beam out the essence, and describe the resulting homogeneity as successful correspondence and cultural exchange.

3

A month after the Indo-Jazz Yatra I found myself sitting with some friends at a beachside café in Goa. I looked up from my plate of Goa curry to see a familiar figure sitting at the next table. He was in an orange shirt and maroon pantaloons, his neck weighed down with pendants. It was the marathon dancer from Bombay.

At the table behind us sat a solitary Indian dressed in a flowered Hawaiian shirt and platform heels. He had his feet up on the chair in front of him to ensure that nobody missed his contemporary footwear.

The Indian leaned across to our table of fellow Indians and raising his eyebrows to indicate the dancer said,

"Look at that fellow over there. He is drugged. That is all they are good for. Drugs and sex. Sex and drugs. I tell you!"

He hitched up his trousers disapprovingly to reveal bright pink socks above the platform heels.

The proprietor of the café came out with a bottle of beer and sat down next to the dancer.

"Have a drink, Ron," he said.

"How's a drink going to help?" said the dancer bitterly. "You know, I am a qualified mechanical engineer. From Toronto, no less, and do you know how long I worked on that bike? Three months! That Enfield was a heap of junk when I bought it, and now it's a work of art. Why else would some Sindhi bloodsucker offer seven thousand rupees for it?"

The Indian with the platform heels interrupted the dancer's passionate tirade.

"What fool will buy a secondhand Enfield for seven thousand rupees? Certainly no one from the Sind, from where I am proud to hail. You are having hallushinashions, my friend. Drink some ice-cold water."

The dancer peered over our heads to locate the cynic seated behind us.

"Who says you know shit about bikes?"

The Sindhi smiled in a superior fashion.

"I know much about motorcycles. I own a garage. My partner competes in the Poona races. Fifty laps around the course, my dear. And I can tell you that no one will pay seven thousand rupees for a secondhand Enfield, no matter what you have done with your so many degrees. Also, your machine will probably not even climb that small little hill over there."

The Canadian pushed back his chair and strode over to tower over his tormentor.

"Is that so, asshole? I ran that bike nonstop from Bombay to Goa yesterday. Eighteen straight hours. That baby's engine didn't even cough."

The dancer ran his eyes in disgust over the Indian lounging back in his chair, to be brought up short by the platform heels. "Holy shit!" he shouted. "Where did you get the leather?"

The Sindhi gave another superior smirk.

"How you people think you are the only ones who can make. Well, these shoes that you are so much admiring have not been sent from foreign. They are made in Bombay bazaar, my dear. Perhaps that will surprise *you*."

He turned to our table, embracing us in the glow of his national pride. The Canadian leaned over the table.

"Bombay bazaar, huh? You could have fooled me. I thought they were from an orthopedic ward."

Platform Heels silently digested the information that the foreigner, far from envying his shoes, was actually sneering at them. He recovered quickly.

"Well sala, at least I am wearing what is made in my own country. And I work for my living like a man. Look at you, in women's clothes. What kind of fool are you looking like may I ask?"

He made a contemptuous gesture that took in the maroon and orange ensemble and the necklaces dangling in front of his eyes.

"Women?" shouted the offended Canadian. "Listen, faggot, where I come from women dress in your kind of shirt. Why don't you stop leering at all the naked honchos on the beach and come take a ride with me on my useless machine?"

"Certainly, sala," said the Sindhi haughtily. "But I will not hold your shoulders. You are a druggie. God alone knows if you can drive with all your big talk. I will drive. You sit on the pillion and give your two-paisa advice to the wind."

The Sindhi and the Canadian set off toward the motorcycle, which was parked in the inadequate shade of a palm tree. We leaned over to see which of them would drive.

Finally the Canadian slammed the keys into the Sindhi's

hands and the Sindhi climbed triumphantly onto the bike and pushed it off its starting block. His platform heels kept getting in the way of the pedal as he attempted to kick it. The Canadian acknowledged each false start with a bow and a wave to the audience looking on from the café. At last Platform Heels got the engine going, the dancer got on behind him, and they disappeared down the road.

Twenty minutes later there was a sound of revving engines and the motorcycle skidded to a halt in front of the café, kicking up sand in everyone's faces. The Sindhi pushed the bike back onto its stand and jumped off excitedly. He threw his arms around the Canadian's shoulder.

"My dear, what a wonderful machine! Better than many in my own garage. Now tell me, how have you done it?"

The Canadian grinned. "Went to Thieves' Bazaar in Bombay. Just happened on a couple of Harley Davidson parts."

The Indian slapped him on the back.

"I should have known. Harley. The prince of engines. Oh, you are a clever chap in spite of your drugs and your pajamas."

The Canadian shouted up to the proprietor,

"Hey man, break out some cold beer for my buddy here."

The orange-clad dancer and the platform-heeled garage owner made their way up the steps of the café, each wearing the other's clothes, deep in discussion of the motorcycle engine.

The danger of men becoming Muzak, a background hum to keep busy machines happy, has not been overlooked in India. In the old days the warrior garlanded his sword, the trader propitiated his scales, an annual reminder that unless the proper distance and respect were maintained between men and the products of their invention, it was possible that the machine might take over.

Today when the season comes for that commemoration, the

offices and factories of India are filled with people garlanding air conditioners, placing coconuts in front of cash registers, and placating computers with fresh fruit. As a· result of these precautions, they are still sometimes able to converse without the intermediary of a machine.

4

In somebody's beach shack that evening we chanced upon a young Indian who lived in New York.

We were sitting on the veranda of an old wooden house, watching the sun set over the Indian Ocean. The Indian was lying on a string hammock and smoking a joint. Near his hammock, a pretty German girl sat cross-legged on the floor.

"How long have you lived in New York?" she asked the Indian.

"About two years," he replied.

"What do you do there?"

"I'm a computer guru."

"What nonsense! You're stoned!"

"I am not," said the Indian indignantly. "I own my own computer company."

"But you're so young. How can you *own* a computer company?"

By this time the sun had set and we felt we should be moving on. The Indian was giggling in his hammock.

"Who wants to hear the story of my life?" he asked the gathering.

"Oh, Gott! You are stoned!" said the German girl accusingly. "When are you kids going to stop dope and start work?"

Screams of laughter came from the hammock. It rocked dangerously. Then a head appeared over the side and addressed us.

"You can't go now. Wait till I tell you how I became a success in America at the age of twenty-two. I shall tell my story quickly. I have plans of spending the night here."

"Oh, Gott," said the German girl, and disappeared to get some tea.

The Indian rolled another joint, the girl came back with the tea tray and we listened.

"My story is about an Indian who managed through family connections to get a job in New York with a computer firm. His only qualifications were a failing grade in mathematics from Bombay University, and two years' training in computer technology."

A suspense story. We all settled down.

"I thought because I had an electric guitar and used to play with a rock group I'd be welcomed in America. Well, I didn't know it was possible to be so lonely.

"I mean, here you have to fight to be alone, don't you? There it's the exact reverse. They call it 'being alienated.'

"Me? I just wanted a friend. So I spent that first year getting stoned with my computer. Those were the only conversations I had."

The German girl was looking at him with a strange expression, sympathy mixed with fear.

"I spent all my time with that machine, program sheet in one hand, joint in the other. Solving problems with my one pal in town.

"Naturally, I got a reputation as a whiz kid. The guy who owned the company was so impressed with me that he set me up on my own to solve specialist computer problems. Now I'm a big success, with lots of friends.

"They call me the computer guru."

The Indian leaned out of his hammock and leered at the German girl sitting on the ground below him.

"The only thing is, I may have to stay stoned forever, see.

"My professional reputation depends on it."

IX

THE ODDS AND
THE GODS

I

A French girl lives under a tree in a jungle behind Delhi University. She has been there nearly seven years. In that time she has borne two children to an Indian holy man. Now the holy man is dead. Her son, first fruit of her union with an Indian ascetic, is dead. She has been charged with murdering them, and has denied the charges not in French but in the flawless Hindustani she has learned during her sojourn in the jungle. The university students are not aware of her presence. The villagers are, but some think she is an incarnation of the Goddess. Others think she is a witch. Or insane.

"I took a vow with my guru that I would remain here seven years. In two months my time will be up. What a seven years it has been. When I first saw the Teacher I couldn't believe my eyes. He was sitting under a tree, a fat oily man listening to a transistor radio. All his disciples sat at his feet adoring him. I thought, what are they doing? This man is a *halwai*, a sweetmeat vendor!"

It was spring in the jungle. All the trees were in leaf. The French girl's blond-haired, dark-skinned daughter skipped from rock to rock over the small stream that ran by the side of the thorn tree, the only home she had ever known. Her mother, wrapped in a thin cotton sarong, squatted by the stream and washed clothes like a village woman, picking the wet things up and striking them hard against the rocks to loosen the dirt.

"Now he's dead. And for months the police believed I had killed him. My guru! My own son! But I'm not scared of the police. I've seen enough of them in my life. It's because of them that I am in India today."

The child was shrieking at the trees, drowning her mother's voice. After each shriek she paused as though expecting a reply from the jungle. She danced toward her mother, explaining over her shoulder,

"I'm calling the peacocks. If they are nearby they'll come to me. I'm their friend."

Her mother put a hand on the child's shoulder and levered herself to a standing position.

"The guru had prepared me to face this trouble. When our son was born he warned me, 'This child is mine. He must come with me when I leave my body, so we may work together in our next incarnation.' I wept but the guru consoled me, 'I shall give you a daughter to comfort you when we are gone. You will need comfort when the world accuses you of killing us.' See where he died. Under this tree."

The French girl walked over to the thorn tree. Her child skipped along barefoot behind her as the soapsuds disappeared in a white slime behind the rocks at the bottom of the clearing.

"This is all that is left of the Master. This trishul and this child. Oh yes, and this green cloth on which we conceived our children and on which he died. Would you say these are worth the lives of the two people you love most in this or any other world?"

She sat down on the green cloth and folded her hands in respect to the trishul, the ascetic's iron trident, driven into the ground in front of the tree.

"But will the police believe you? Never! They say you are a foreigner, living in the jungle. You must be the murderess. If you are not, prove it.

"What can I prove? The Master lay down one night, closed his eyes, and never opened them again. As he took his last breath, my son, hardly a year old, sat up, folded his hands to his father's trident, and fell back dead. I screamed and fainted, my daughter in my arms. The next day the police came. They sat around this tree day and night for three weeks. Jealous disciples had told them I had poisoned the Master.

"I was destroyed with grief and the fever, and my daughter, a two-month-old baby feeding at my breast, whether I was conscious or unconscious.

"Sometimes a kind villager made me drink some water or some daal soup. Otherwise I too would have died. Finally, the police decided that I could be innocent. So they went away.

"What a tamasha, hey, Haran? When they thought I was a murderess?"

The French girl laughed and waved at a large muscular young Indian who had suddenly appeared at the far end of the clearing. The Indian's hair fell to his shoulders and his beard to his chest. He wore a red quilted vest over his naked shoulders and an amulet against the evil eye on a black string around his neck. He nodded absently at the French girl and disappeared behind a tree. When he reappeared he had changed his faded Levi's for a green-and-yellow striped sarong.

"It all began with my mother in France. She was *la vrai bourgeoise*, always worried about the neighbors. She cared more about them than about me, so I ran away. I got a job as a groom in a rich man's stable. One night he tried to seduce me. But I'm not that kind of girl. I ran away again. He told my mother and Interpol that I had stolen a lot of money from him, with a gun. I ran all the way to Turkey. There I met some people in a tea stall who were leaving for India. Well, they managed to get me a visa, and I thought India is a big country, even Interpol won't find me here."

The Indian was sitting cross-legged on the ground. In front of him was a cotton bandana on which were placed several pouches. He was transferring small paper packets from one pouch to the other. Each time he moved a packet there was a roll of powerful muscles from his neck to his wrists.

"Once I got to India I left the Europeans, because they only talked of drugs. But some spoke of gurus. They say in India the holy men are to be found in the mountains. I put all my belongings in a bag and set off for the mountains to find a guru. I had no money, but I was fed at the temples and slept in the fields.

"I remember I was in the holy city of Hardwar, standing by the river. I looked down and saw that in one hand I carried my passport, the guarantee of the President of France that I was free to travel anywhere in the world. But where was I to go? In my other hand I carried my mala. Those beads were also a passport, to the ways of the spirit. I could only follow one of them.

"I chose and threw my passport into the river. As the passport hit the water, will you believe this? From those very ripples appeared the face of my guru, laughing and calling my name.

"I knew then that I had chosen the right path, and I began my real search for the Teacher."

2

To the thousands and thousands of the French girl's compatriots living in seedy hotels all over India, such behavior would be dismissed as naiveté or insanity.

Why fling the passport into the river, especially when it had so many unstamped visa pages? She could have sold it and at a good price. The resale value of a passport goes up in geometric proportion to the number of blank visa pages. If she had just waited until she got to Connaught Place in downtown New Delhi she would have been able to complete the transaction in a matter of minutes. Then she could have gone to the French Embassy, reported the theft of her passport, and got herself a brand-new *laissez-passer*, just in case the mala had misled her and the guru's smiling face turned out to be a fantasy of her tired brain.

Eighty percent of the illegal passport trade between French citizens in Asia takes place, not as might be supposed in the old French colonies of Indochina and the countries surrounding them, but in New Delhi's Connaught Place. The black market in travel documents is not limited to the French. It is a going business for papers from most Western countries, whose Consular Corps distractedly watch illegal passports being flung all over the subcontinent like confetti at a masked ball. The elegant diplomats find less and less of their working day is spent in exchanging bon mots and bonbons with one another, and more and more of it goes in protecting themselves from this constantly expanding underworld.

One consul had smiled grimly at me across the four feet that separated his desk from my chair, four feet of no-man's-land, a monument to the changing times. He had joined the diplomatic service to live a life as formal and as tightly ordained as the Court at Versailles, and found himself reduced to creating enough physical space to avoid contracting the diseases and the body lice of his fellow citizens.

"It is an evil world today, Madame. Last week a young couple came in here. They were sitting exactly where you sit now. They were very excited. They had lost their passports. I gave them new *laissez-passer*. But they didn't go away. Instead they walked up to my desk and laid a bundle wrapped in rags in front of me.

"'What is it?' I asked them.

"'It is our son,' they replied.

"'Is he sick?' I asked.

"'No, monsieur. He is dead.' Then they said to me,

"'Bury him.'

"'I have no funds to bury babies, Madame. I cannot just demand from a foreign government space in a graveyard for an unknown body.'

"'Then bury him in France,' they told me.

"'He is a citizen of France!'

"They had no proof that they were the parents. But I felt sorry for them in their bereavement, so I took some money from my own pocket and told them to go to the cremation grounds.

"'Have the body burnt,' I advised. 'This money will pay for it.'

"They were very happy. They took the bundle, their new papers, my money, and they went away shouting 'Vive La France!' Even to the Indian watchman.

"The next morning I received a telephone call from the crematorium. They asked,

"'Are you the French Consul?'

"'Oui. Yes, it is me,' I said.

"They said to me, "'There is the body of a dead child lying in front of our gates. What shall we do with it?'

"I was very busy. I could not understand why they were calling me.

"'Why don't you burn it? You are a crematorium. Dead bodies are your business, not the business of the Embassy of France!'

"'Not this one,' they told me. 'There is a paper pinned to the body, addressed to you.'

"'Addressed to me?'

"'Yes. It says, A Present for the French Consul.'

"What can I say, Madame? What kind of world do we live in? Where parents sell the dead bodies of their own children for cash! And what will they do with the cash? Buy drugs. Some to use, some to sell to other unfortunates like themselves.

"We have told your government, all of us from the Embassies, so many times. Your government shrugs. The officials say these are our citizens, we must look after them."

3

The passport rackets finance the drug trade, and it's the drugs that earn the big bucks, and everyone knows that where there are big bucks there's a lot of action. When the French girl arrived in India all those years ago she regularly smoked hashish and opium.

"Now I only use drugs for religious purposes, to help me go into a trance. In fact, I was in that kind of spiritual trance in a temple in Benares when a beggar told me of a Teacher in a jungle outside Delhi who was waiting for a white woman who would be the greatest of his followers. I knew this was a message. The Teacher had tested my endurance long enough. I left the temple immediately and went to Delhi."

The French girl interrupted her narrative to acknowledge the presence of a new arrival. A well-dressed European who looked to be in his late sixties was waving at her from across the stream.

"Viens ici! Viens ici!" shouted the girl. The man stared dubiously at the puddles near his shining black shoes, and adjusted the cameras slung over his shoulders. The girl counseled him to jump. She called for her child. The child appeared from behind a tree, the man successfully landed on dry ground, and the Indian tied up his pouches and stowed the bundle behind his back.

The newcomer was introduced as a stockbroker who had come

to take photographs of the French girl and her child, for the girl's mother back in France.

"My mother wants pictures of me now. You know why? The Mother of Pondicherry is dead, and there are people who think I should take her place. She was French. I am French. A few talent scouts from the ashram have been to see me. After all, Auroville is more than an ashram. It is a whole city, with money from governments and the United Nations and so many donations. To continue they must find a successor. The French press is very excited, journalists have visited me. And my mother wants photographs of me now. She thinks I will be famous. Like a Pope!"

As she spoke, the French girl dressed her child in a red silk skirt. Then she sat the child on her lap and began combing the child's hair with a fine-toothed delousing comb. The stockbroker was clicking away with his cameras, shooting roll upon roll of candid exposure. Suddenly, the child tugged at her mother's sarong and succeeded in freeing one withered breast. The stockbroker looked alarmed and put down his cameras. The French girl continued to inspect her child's head for lice, the child with a full set of milk teeth continued to suck at her mother's milkless breast, unperturbed by their audience.

The stockbroker put his cameras back into their case, bowed stiffly to the French girl, and left. The girl laughed,

"I am not going to be the new Frenchwoman to take over the Auroville empire in Pondicherry. I have been here nearly seven years. When my time is up, my daughter and I will move on. I may give up the religious life. Move to Benares. I believe Benares is amusant now."

The Indian coughed discreetly.

4

Benares is daily getting more amusant.

It is the city on the banks of the River Ganges at its most holy confluence. The heart of Hindu India, with the paradoxes laid out in perfect sequence. First the river: mortality and immortality. Then the temples: piety and profanity. Then the bazaars: commerce and charity. Then the beggars: poverty and sanctity.

"Look, honey," said the troubleshooter at the American Embassy. "I can't see you this afternoon. One of our guys pulled out a gun and shot another one of our guys dead in a temple just outside Benares. Probably fighting over dope, but I gotta get up there and sort it out. Let's get together when I get back, okay?"

It was from this city that the brocade route originated, its craftsmen carrying to Nepal, Tibet and China not just their knowledge of silks and weaving, but also the secrets of Hindu learning, until the largest expanse of land and people on earth had heard and accepted the concepts of reincarnation and Moksha, release.

"You don't really want to see what's become of Benares in the last few years," said the German photographer. "Everywhere now you find morphine. Sores on the arms. People dying on the streets."

It is the city where widows go from the conservative Hindu enclaves which look upon marrying a widow as an obscenity matched only by necrophilia. In their white saris and with their shaven heads the widows can be seen at every temple, begging alms from the pilgrims who come to offer prayers for their ancestors.

Other mendicants are sadhus down from the mountains, naked and carrying the iron trident to show their allegiance to the god Shiva. Some beggars are practitioners of Tantra, searching to realize the nonexistence of good and evil, breaking the taboos of caste by begging from those of any caste. Others are hippies, taking survival the easy way.

The original hippies were more than beggars. They were pathfinders who discovered the burning ghats. India is probably the only country in the world that allows the tourist to treat death as a spectator sport, and nowadays tourists increasingly look to India for the experience. Trips to the unknown are monogrammed by the sensation not the photograph, and few places are more sensational than the burning ghats at Benares—the place where all devout Hindus hope to be cremated.

Inevitably, those who perform the cremations have a stranglehold on the devout and some use their power mercilessly. Priests bargain with bereaved families over the price and the quantity of sandalwood and clarified butter to be used for the funeral pyre, to help ignition and salvation. Battles are fought over the price of each verse of the holy Sanskrit scriptures to be recited while the body burns. And when the negotiations finally draw to a halt, and the body is successfully burning, and the head of the corpse has exploded, then further bargaining begins. The price of the guard who will watch over the body until it is reduced to ashes, a necessary expense because among the large number of sadhus at the ghats there might be some who are trying to rise above conventional morals by eating human flesh.

The hippies found Benares more than just a good place to beg. It was also the best place to get stoned and freak out on eternity. In the early days, the hippies used the simple joint to induce philosophy. They spent many pleasant hours at the burning ghats, watching the smoke from the funeral pyres unite with the smoke from their joints, the fumes spiraling upwards to the vultures circling in the hot Indian sky. Metaphors of living and dying and India.

Lately these visions of death and its marketplace have not been sufficient to entertain the growing number of voyeurs. People are demanding something more to heighten their experience of experience.

"It's the needle. The needle has replaced the pipe. There's enough happening in Benares without that. Why don't you people do something?" asked the Dutch sociologist shortly before he began casting the I Ching.

"Don't you know once that starts it is carried on by its own momentum?"

The sociologist has a case. The service industries for the sophisticated tourist are being run by increasingly sophisticated professionals. Some have come to India because their lucrative trade in Indochina was another casualty of the Vietnam war. Others have come because it is getting harder to get raw opium out of Turkey and the Golden Triangle, whereas the Indian subcontinent grows more opium than any country in the world.

In fact there was a time when the trade of the entire Western World rested on the fragile back of the white poppy of India, the seeds brought from Asia Minor by the Moghul emperors, the fields exploited by British merchants.

The British pried open the gates of Imperial China with tea and then debauched that Empire with Indian opium in order to keep those gates open, first by smuggling and then by gunboats, leading to the thirty-odd years of conflict which the embittered and addicted Chinese were to call The Opium Wars.

The Americans, finding the opium they brought from Turkey too inferior for the tastes of the addicts of China, turned to the opium fields of India for the invaluable poppy that would guarantee the Chinese silver that America needed to keep alive the boast of "the silver dollar."

The British East India Company used opium to spread decay among the spinning wheel and handloom craftsmen of India, so that Indian weavers would tend the poppy fields not their looms, and be forced to buy the manufactured textiles of the steam-powered Lancashire mills.

The Dutch used opium to break down the resistance of the Indonesians to the semislavery of the Dutch East India Company's profit-making plantations.

The French traded in opium. The Portuguese traded in opium.

And the British merchant houses who had made their fortunes in the East did not ignore their own. By the nineteenth century, opium was being taken in Great Britain, not just by avant-garde writers, but by the vast majority of those North of England workers who kept the wheels of the Industrial Revolution turning, and for whom it was a cheaper and more available consciousness killer than beer or gin.

Two hundred years later, through the tortuous route of history and philosophy, the dealers are back in India. Without the moral and military backing of their governments, it is true. But with the gains of the Industrial Revolution, which have replaced the handmade pipe with the factory-turned hypodermic.

Despite the illegality, the drug traders of Benares seem to feel little need for secrecy. They have scouts operating more or less openly in the hotels of the big cities and the tourist traps around the country. In less than a decade Benares has become a haven for chemists and dealers who have drifted into the city from all over the world. Most of these professionals are still non-Indian, although it is only a question of for how long. It is unlikely that Indians will continue to be content by only providing the floorshow, with their dead and their bereaved.

Meanwhile, Delhi is hosting yet another international conference, this time on the problems and solutions to international drug-peddling. India prides herself on having the best record on controlling illegal drug traffic in the world. While the bureaucrats congratulate themselves on the efficacy of their controls, the drug traffic grows and grows, and Benares looks set on replacing Bangkok as Needle City, Asia.

5

"But I'm not scared of the police," the French girl had said. "It's because of them that I'm in India today."

Whatever the origins of her visit, India has given the French girl a number of attractive options.

If she holds to her plan to revisit Benares, she will find a larger variety of spiritual stimulants available to her than was available seven years ago. When she wishes to go into a religious trance at the burning ghats, she will find it easier to do so. Systems, efficiency, and time and motion studies have been put into operation while she was under her thorn tree.

The Hindu element remains constant. The corpse carriers continue to bring their cargoes of dead bodies for the funeral pyres, and they still chant,

Ram Nam Sat Hai, Ram Nam Sat Hai.
The Name of God is Truth.

But the trance-inducing industry has improved. Now the dope, hard and soft, is available from houseboats. The houseboats have been moored on the holy river in the immediate vicinity of the burning ghats. Thus, customers are provided with easy and constant access to both death and delirium.

Or the French girl could change her mind and reconsider the possibility of becoming a religious leader. There's little chance that she would be acceptable to the Auroville ashram, but for her, it's a reasonable gamble. If the ashram did vote her their girl, she would have sole control over the hearts and fortunes of a large and wealthy religious community.

Or she could go to her embassy and apply for a new passport, which she could then sell to raise enough money to set up as a small drugs entrepreneur, financing smuggling operations either West to Amsterdam and Marseilles, in finished goods, or else sending raw opium East to Hong Kong to be refined and adulterated into Chinese heroin, which the Chinese will resell to the West.

Interpol may yet catch up with her, though the odds are against it. If they do, immediately closing all her options in one fell swoop, then depending on which culture she's currently coming from,
That's either karma.
Or it's showbiz.

X

SEX AND THE
SINGLES GURU

I

There are several ashrams in vogue in India where marriage is considered bourgeois.

The more sophisticated devotees in these ashrams are prepared to enter the erstwhile "holy" state just to beat the system. They will marry Indians trying to get into Canada, the United States, or the United Kingdom who have been unable to pass through bureaucratic channels, to show their contempt for bureaucracy. Others are inspired less by liberation than by cupidity, and charge cash money for the marriage license. Either way, at the end of the ceremonies and the paperwork, the outsiders feel a little closer to the real India, and the Indians wing their way to the real West. Some Indians, however, come to the ashrams not as a way of going West, but simply as a ruse to get closer to desirable Westerners.

One afternoon I was grateful to be sitting in the cool white marble splendor of an ashram air-conditioned by the funds of thousands of foreign devotees. I was in the ashram head office, run by an older Indian woman considered almost an embodiment of the guru. The guru was inaccessible except at matins and vespers, so for the rest of the day the devotees drew succor from his proxy, or as some cynics had it, his doxy.

The devotees were not cynics. They adored the woman and loved tending her. During my visit she sat behind a huge desk in a room with glass walls on three sides. Each wall gave onto a pleasant prospect. Beyond one wall was a path lined with bougainvillea bushes cascading their bright flowers over the red earth. Through another was visible the ashram's favorite folly, half-maze half-water, in which wandered the ashram inmates holding hands and absorbing the energy of plants and sky. The third wall looked onto corridors, partitioned with tables where the ashram bookkeepers and accountants and brochure designers and magazine editors and incense producers and club managers and like that, were hard at work.

The guru's number two sat behind her desk on a leather chair, presiding over the pious. The pious exhibited their piety in a number of ways. One man sat under the woman's desk in the lotus position. Where his calves crossed the devotee had placed a cushion. On this cushion he was tenderly guarding the woman's left foot. Being rather large, the devotee was unable to sit straight and was listing forward dangerously toward the filing cabinets at the end of the desk.

The obvious discomfort of his physical state did not deflect him from his chosen task of devotion, which appeared to the untrained eye to be that of giving the woman, whom he called Ma, a pedicure. Every now and then Ma would bend under the desk and pat any part of the devotee's anatomy that was immediately available for benediction. The pedicurist was holed up under the desk for these moments, and if in a tremble of delight he clipped Ma a little too closely, Ma would give a mock scream, everyone would laugh, and then Ma would return to the business at hand.

But only at one hand, because her left hand was being looked after by another devotee. Ma's shoulders were being massaged by a third devotee, and more devotees kept entering the room just to pluck at the hem of her garment and go out again. I couldn't see any means of showing my goodwill in this spiritual beauty parlor, as everything short of plucking Ma's eyebrows was already being attended to, and others were queuing up behind the attendants, waiting to take their place.

Meanwhile Ma was on the telephone, talking to the land-distribution officer at the city's head office, the Secretary of the Finance Ministry in the state capitol, and officials at the External Affairs Ministry in New Delhi. All these long and short distance calls were put through on her multi-line telephone by an abject operator, who sat in the corridor and waved at Ma through the glass partition. Sometimes Ma would remember to wave back. Waist deep in devotion Ma spoke into the telephone, juggling the ashram's large fortune and dicey reputation, taking the role of the humble, uneducated Hindu woman with one caller, the arrogant spiritual leader with another, and the flirtatious woman of the world to a third.

In the middle of all this, a flustered Parsi woman burst into the room, and dived under the desk to touch Ma's feet. The devotees waiting outside the office cried it wasn't their fault. The pedicurist took fright and inadvertently cut Ma's toes. Ma was furious but controlled herself. Everyone looked with disgust at the Parsi woman.

An older, harassed creature, she was obviously the ashram's weak link. But the guru had recognized her genuine devotion and permitted her to officiate one afternoon a week at the ashram bookstall, which stood just inside the impressive marble gates at the ashram's entrance.

It was at the bookstall that the Parsi woman's problems had originated. Every day for the last three weeks a young sardar had come to the bookstall to buy literature on the ashram. He had also purchased up to volume forty-three of the guru's prodigious output. After buying the books, he would disappear into the ashram for a couple of hours, and the Parsi woman would smile to herself, knowing another soul was about to join the community. This afternoon she had learned that the Sikh's motives had not been spiritual at all. He was spending all his money on holy books because he longed for the narrow hips and heavy breasts of an Australian nymphet.

After three weeks of chitchat on Being, Cosmic Energy, and Going Toward Yourself, the youth's lust, straining too long against his trousers, could contain itself no longer. He had, in the middle of a conversation about Primal Screaming as a means of getting back in contact with the body, thrown the nymphet under the nearest bougainvillea bush and attempted to get in touch with her body without any philosophical preliminaries. The nymphet had proved extremely uncooperative and made a fight of it. This had attracted the attention of several ashram devotees, who had pulled the Sikh by his long hair off her body and dragged him out of the ashram gates, which they had firmly barred to him. He was now standing with his face pressed against the bookshop window, screaming, "Get the Guru. Tell him I must become a devotee now! It's very urgent!"

The Parsi woman, horrified by the exhibition of naked lust, had rushed to Ma's office for a solution.

Ma's eyes narrowed as the woman told her disjointed tale. Ma removed her extremities from the ministrations of the faithful, and picked up her mala—the sign that she wanted quiet. The room was silent while Ma thought. In a minute Ma smiled and we all followed suit.

"If he wants to be near the girl, that's beautiful. He will be made a member of the ashram at the evening devotions when Swami initiates the new devotees."

The Parsi woman touched Ma's feet in relief and went out into the sun with her message for the importunate sardar. There was a general relaxing of tension.

A twenty-year-old girl who had been standing in the office through the entire episode suddenly climbed onto Ma's lap. She curled a lock of Ma's hair around her finger and crooned, "You're our Mummy. That's what you are. Mu . . . . mmmmm . . . . . eeeeee."

It was quick thinking on Ma's part. Already the ashram was getting a reputation for orgies and the local population kept an eye on what was going on. The devotees were forced to screen people attending the morning devotions and separate the rich voyeurs who would donate, from the sort of people who would make a fuss with the authorities because they felt their religion was being insulted.

Ma had grasped immediately that a young Sikh in love might create a lot of trouble with the authorities. Rather than fight him she had allowed him to join. He was an exception for Indians— the guru's teachings on sex had made that clear.

2

The waves of mother love at the ashram had become too much for me. I slunk out of the ashram's back gate, pushing my way through mounds of shining paper—printed material and shredded posters. This was the excess from the ashram's printing and publishing ventures, which were both in design and quality of a much higher standard than anything available in Indian shops.

A sweeper woman was standing with a large cane basket at the gate, sweeping the paper into her basket with a broom made of dried rushes. I stopped to watch her.

"Are you going to sell the paper by weight?" I asked.

"That's the only way I can sell it. I soak it in water and sell it in the bazaar down the road," she said.

A lovely red-haired girl was walking down the road toward us. She stroked the hedges lasciviously with her hands, running her bare arms along the bushes despite the thorns.

"See they cut it up so small with their foreign machines that we can't even sell it to the peanut men or the split-pea men. Not a single piece of paper is large enough to hold even five paisa's worth of nuts," the sweeper continued.

The girl had paused and was swaying her body sinuously at a jacaranda tree, her eyes half-closed, her strong well-shaped body clearly visible through the flimsy cotton she had wrapped around herself as a sarong.

"What is she doing?" I asked.

"Bathing in the guru's energy," said the sweeper woman.

"The guru's energy? But where is he?" I demanded.

"He lives in a house behind those trees. These people believe his shakti is so strong that it goes through the walls."

The girl was weaving her way toward us. The sweeper woman contemplated her.

"I should take this one home for my husband. Maybe he would give me a little peace."

"Don't you believe in the guru?" I asked.

"No, sister. I don't believe in the guru. He is playing games with these people. Look at this girl. Has he given her peace or has he just made her desire stronger?

"I tell you, sister. These days I have only one god. The Municipal Corporation."

3

The guru of the ashram had said there is a distinct difference between the Indian attitude toward sex and the Western attitude toward it, a difference that required completely separate forms of meditation. The guru stated that foreigners still had an adolescent approach to sex, stemming from the society to which they had been born: a society that was deeply competitive and one in which the upheavals of the sexual revolution had only succeeded in accentuating sexual competition. His conclusion, which the ashram inmates gratefully accepted, was that the Westerner has a profound fear of impotence, and an equally profound terror of that feeling of impotence becoming common knowledge, making him an object of derision.

The guru exhorted his disciples to overcome their fear by any means they wished, which included for the Western disciples the option of acting out all their sexual fantasies until they exorcised them. The guru quoted freely from the works of Freud and Jung. Few of the disciples knew the works of either thinker outside the popular clichés, so the guru had a certain latitude for interpretation.

"There is no sin but self-loathing. The Self is God. If you loathe your body you loathe yourself. Go toward your body, go toward your desire, and then go *past* them. The death of desire is the birth of Atman."

Other gurus who attempted to teach the same principle were not quite so progressive. One guru who had stated at a lecture that his disciples must learn love, that they must release the love

155

mechanism in themselves by any trigger available, that they must love him as a father, a mother, a brother, a lover, a husband, to reach knowledge of his Godhead, was thunderstruck when he was taken literally and a young American woman burst into his room one night screaming,

"Take me, Lover! I'm yours!"

The guru had her forcibly removed from his bedroom and thrown out of the ashram. She sits outside the ashram gates waiting for the guru to relent. It has been over two years since she got the guru's lecture wrong. The guru meanwhile has surrounded himself with a Praetorian Guard of pure young men whose duty it is to prevent a recurrence of such ardor. The guru is now suspected of harboring homosexual proclivities.

His progressive colleague uses another deterrent—economics. He maintains that the Indian as always suffers from inadequate supply, this time, of sex. He just cannot get enough. He has to be reminded over and over that enough is never quite enough, that appetite is greedy for appetite, that desire generates desire. So the Indian does not need to participate in the elaborate techniques designed by the ashram to help the foreigner get over his fear of impotence.

These categories are convenient for the guru. It enables him to personally screen any Indians who try to get into the sex-therapy meditations on the grounds that he as their teacher, and indeed their God, is directly responsible for their welfare and must himself decide whether each Indian's involvement with adolescent sexual behavior will be a help or a hindrance in spiritual development. It is one way of preventing the ashram from being overrun by horny Indians. It also helps keep the police off the guru's back.

The guru is banking on the Indians' indifference to what foreigners do among themselves, and the only Indians who are allowed to bask in the warmth of the ashram's sexual liberation are those who have a vested interest in maintaining the discretion.

4

Teachers of Tantra, the philosophy that is most intimately concerned with sex of all the Hindu disciplines, have teetered on the edge of social acceptance in India for several hundred years for using sex and death as their basic metaphors, much as gold was used as the metaphor for the secret teachings of alchemy. The Tantrics believe that perfect synthesis—because it cancels out time and space—allows the human mind to perceive eternity in the present. They say it is possible for the truly aware man to realize this synthesis in sexual union or in physical communion with death.

The Tantrics believe in danger. Their teachings are revealed wisdom, shrouded in the rituals of secrecy. In Western mythology, the alchemist's greed for the magic property that turned base metals into gold might lead the alchemist into a pact with the devil. In Tantra the untrained disciple may find himself with a severe case of death hypnosis or sex hypnosis, unable to escape the vortex of sensuality for the negations of immortality.

The Tantrics would be surprised to learn that the taboos that they believe should only be broken by the initiate, lest they boomerang against the practitioner, are now being used as a means of getting rid of one's hang-ups. And of ensuring that one's children have no hang-ups at all.

There is a branch of Tantra in Nepal where a five or six-year-old girl child is chosen as an incarnation of the Goddess. From the moment she is taken from her family she becomes an incarnation of the Goddess, and remains an incarnate until she reaches puberty. Then she ceases to be holy and her descent to humanity is softened by a lifetime pension for herself and her family.

If at any point she loses her virginity, by marriage or by any other means, the pension is immediately withdrawn. It is a curious spinsterhood, but under the economic considerations— she is often the sole support of her destitute family which converge to ensure her continued sanctity—is an understanding that ritual must at all times be fueled by myth. The myth in this case is the two aspects of the Goddess, the benign Mother, and the savage Female principle whose appetites cannot be sated even by the blood of her own young.

Having once worn the mantle of Transcendence, the Goddess as the source of life, the child is prohibited from indulging her sensuality: she may not procreate because she is Creation, and has been revered as the mystery.

No one climbs on her lap saying, "You are our mummy." Not even twenty-year-old women who have children themselves.

5

To the eastern mind, one of the curious aspects of Western liberation is how quickly new techniques and experiments are imposed upon the children, in a desperate attempt to break the holds of heredity. In the ashrams, too, the Western disciples are attempting to ensure that the sins of the fathers are not visited on the children. They impose their newly found freedoms on their children, and then retire to the guru's lap physically or metaphorically while the children are left to sink or swim. Frequently parents leave children at home with a perplexed relative while they come to India to work through their fears of impotence or isolation. These children, although now of one-parent or no-parent families, are often better off than the children in the ashrams, fruits of liberation, products of an all-parent family.

"The kids are marvelous. They do it whenever they feel like."

"The children have no hang-ups. Sex is perfectly *natural* for them."

"That little seven year old is a real Lolita. She's the best lay in the ashram."

"We learn so much from them. Especially in their attitudes to sex. They teach us how to be one with our bodies."

Unfortunately, whatever their claims to immortality, the gurus will pass on. The huge cults that they rule, thanks to the miracles of jet travel and instant marketing, are a one-generation spectacle that could be brought to an unexpected halt by death or irate governments. Which means that one day these children will have to return to their parents' countries and the nursery systems of the West. Outside the ashram's rarefied atmosphere, the children may find that it would have been easier for them to pay for the sins of their fathers than for their fathers' virtues.

6

Sometimes the fathers pay for not having any idea of what's going on. That was the unfortunate experience of a student from Boston who had been studying to be a rabbi until he found a guru in Nepal. The boy had seen some ugly things in Vietnam, but his response to the horrors of Asia was the standard Western one: the plight of the children really moved him.

One day the rabbi manqué happened to be near a temple outside Katmandu when a man brought his daughter to the temple to beg. The mendicant's daughter was six years old, naked with matted hair that fell in knots to her scarred shoulders. Through each cheek her father had inserted an iron nail. There were scars down the front of her body and her back was crisscrossed with the marks of the lash. Her father carried a whip made of rope to which were attached the blades of small knives, sticking out of a cloth bag slung on his shoulders, together with the rest of his worldly possessions.

The father led the child by a rope tied to her neck. Outside the temple when a sufficiently large crowd had collected, he took the whip out of his bag and flayed the child. People flung money at them in recognition of their asceticism and in respect for the child, who everybody realized would be reborn a saint for the penances she was undergoing in this life.

The American was horrified by this spectacle of cruelty and superstition. He promptly took out his money belt and bought the child from her father. The father couldn't believe his luck. Not only was he getting rid of a mouth to feed, even if it did earn their food, but he was· being offered a handsome sum of money—enough to buy a field back in the village where his brothers had stolen his land, enough to put an end to the flight from starvation, the whimperings of his wounded and hungry child. The father didn't stop to bargain in case the eccentric foreigner thought better of his rash offer. He handed over the child, took the money and ran down the road.

The would-be rabbi took the little girl back to the two-storied house with carved wooden balconies, which he and other visiting students of Tantra had rented from an absentee Nepalese noble. Among the American's fellow residents was a Frenchwoman who had five years of medical school. She and the American were very much in love.

The Frenchwoman immediately flung herself as equal partner into the American's rescue mission. Between them and a lot of antiseptic they managed to get the girl cleaned up and successfully removed the nails from her cheeks. There were added problems. Body lice and malnutrition. But a few good shampoos with lye solved one problem and they knew that only time and wholesome meals would solve the other. The Good Samaritans were less sure they knew how to heal the scars on her soul. They thought perhaps love and understanding would wipe away the ugly memories.

The condition of the child's soul continued to exercise them for some time. The last three years to be exact. Now the American and the Frenchwoman cannot wait to get rid of the child. The American cannot understand what happened to all the innocence that he knows is deep down inside every child. Every time he enters the house, to his horror she tries to give him a blow job. The child cannot believe that he did not buy her for this purpose. She has had extensive experience of holy men and knows they need help on this thorny issue. The American has become more or less celibate as a result of the child's eagerness to please him sexually. The French medical student has naturally taken exception to this celibacy, as she and the rabbinical student were in bliss spiritually and physically before the American's act of spontaneous generosity. The Frenchwoman finds herself in the unsatisfactory position of having neither her sexual feelings reciprocated by her lover, nor her maternal feelings responded to by the child.

When the child is not attempting to pleasure her benefactor, she is out in the streets with a gang of urchins whom she leads in daring feats of theft. She always offers her benefactor first choice over the gang's acquisitions and cannot understand why he will not accept them. It is a battle of wits between the American and the child. The child is winning. She is determined to teach him the necessities of both sex and survival. He is equally determined to teach her conventional morality, and now is on the verge of throwing her, and his moral responsibility to her, out of his house.

Yet everything that the Frenchwoman and the American are learning from their Tantric guru—that the world and good and evil are mere illusion—indicates that the child is the one who has really understood the nature of the ephemeral world and that they are the laggards, still trying to impose a vision of morality, which they maintain they no longer have, in a world where it has become inapplicable.

7

Confusions about morality appear—at least in India—to be one of the side effects of the Second Vatican Council. These confusions have led to a number of nuns and priests eschewing the Christian religion and taking up Hinduism, or else taking a sabbatical from Christianity to follow Indian gurus, in an attempt to discover more about their own consciences.

For four years I was a resident student at a convent, banned from reading books frowned on by the Church, making sure my gym slip hung below my knees. The same nuns who ruled over my spiritual and physical well-being with rods of iron have now opened a branch of their convent down the road from a progressive ashram, to deal with the ashram's fallout. The nuns have their hands busy saving people from the sin of despair or prospect of madness, so severely spiritually wounded are those who ring the bell on the convent door.

But the exalted position of nuns in general is beginning to be compromised in the community. Some of their own number are deserting convents and joining the ashrams. The nuns, like so many other recipients of Pope John's encyclicals, are perplexed by the dictates of the inner voice. When the inner voice ceased to be monitored by the Vatican and became an object of conscience, it created all sorts of problems for the previously quite straightforward vocation. In a land of exploding populations, the nuns found it more and more difficult to counsel abstinence as the best form of family planning. When they shed the protection of the medieval cowls and veils, they found that in their saris, Indians could not distinguish between them and the hippy women similarly dressed. In fact, Indians thought they were madder than the hippies because they were older.

And they found they were no longer isolated from the gibes of certain progressive Indian gurus who paid homage to their piety, but sneered at it as a poor piety that rejected what it had not experienced, a piety based on a retreat from speculative sin. Some of the nuns had been seduced by these suggestions and jumped the wall.

The escapees who found their way to the more progressive ashrams discovered that they occupied a special position both as love objects and as proselytizers. In an ashram, even in one where sex is a common meditation, there is something special about being allowed to fornicate with a nun—especially as the people who are allowed into the meditations are foreigners from a Christian, and often specifically Roman Catholic, background. For them the act of sleeping with a nun is to break the final taboo. The nuns, on their part, are anxious to rid themselves of the burden of ego, which the guru tells them they adopted with their Christian vows, and to learn something about the experiences that they have till now foregone.

So the irresistible force of Hinduism and the immovable

dogma of Christianity find themselves in the therapy rooms, and inevitably something gives. Usually the nun's sense of reality.

In the epic Hindu poem the *Ramayana*, Sita the perfect Hindu woman, is left by her husband's younger brother in the forest to wait while he looks for her lost husband and his king. He draws a line around the anxious wife exhorting her not to step beyond it. His protection is only valid while she remains inside the circle, a barrier to the dangers outside. But Sita sees a golden deer breaking through the undergrowth, calling in her husband's voice. Because her desire to believe is so strong, Sita follows the deer and falls into the grasp of the king of the underworld. The Sanskrit couplet comments,

When the times are bad
The mind is moved to madness.

Once the nuns, in pursuit of a richer spirituality, cross the barriers their vocation imposed on them, they seem compelled to tell the world of their experiences and attack the inhibitions of other nuns.

The sisterhood from the convent feel they should be present at the apostate's harangues, to prove the fallacy of her attacks—a new martyrdom for a new era.

. It was unnerving to hear the same nuns who once a year had given a highly secret lecture for Christians only on the ways of the marriage bed, now coping with the public pillorying they were getting at the hands of one of their own.

"My dear, we are all accused of being Lesbians. Or frustrated old women. The things those young people say to us!"

Full of dark and unexpressed passions. Masochists beating themselves at dawn with whips. Sinners given to self-abuse in the secret of their cells.

At least the nuns and the genuine teachers of Tantra would

have had certain experiences in common. They would both have heard of the dark night of the soul. But how can either defend themselves against the gibes of those who do not believe there is a pain or a pleasure beyond the physical.

8

In the ashrams, those preoccupied with the physical nature of experience also have confusions to overcome. Their own restlessness to translate precept into practice creates much of the confusion. They find that brooding on the paradox is not nearly so enjoyable as being out in the world experiencing it. Being *productive* with enlightenment, as it were. When the paradox has to do with the physical, as in the case of sexuality, the devotees undergo even greater confusion.

If the progressive guru was right that many foreigners come to India wounded in their sex, needing reassurance and freedom of sexual experience to remove their sense of impotence, he has obviously not observed that a fair number of them come to him because they are no longer sure what sex they are.

Among the most serious perceptions of Tantra is the issue of androgyny, and the guru teaches these perceptions without understanding what they mean to his international disciples.

The lines that protect the backward Indian from worrying about the object of his lust and allow him to concentrate on the problem of lust itself do not exist for the Occidental.

When the guru counsels his Western devotees to meditate on their dual sexuality, they frequently interpret his words as a command to become homosexual. The methods that the guru has devised to emphasize the duality seem to reinforce the general schizophrenia and confusion, not alleviate it.

The men who have been on the cooking detail for the last three months or minding the babies or doing all the other tasks that the guru thinks are indicative of passivity, misunderstand the lesson. They think they are supposed to be searching for their homosexual selves. The Female element in the Male they understand only as a sexual simile. The women are guilty of the same misinterpretation, and take the teachings on the Male Principle as an indication that they should try harder to be butch.

No one understands what the guru thinks he is teaching, and he only comes out of chambers twice a day to see them as a group of people who hang on his every word. From their expressions of bliss, he thinks they must have grasped his meaning.

He does not know that most of the disciples are less concerned with the meaning than with the game.

XI

COWBOYS AND
INDIANS

1

A young Indian woman of "good family" was terrified when six Delhi constables arrived at her parents' house at three o'clock in the morning to arrest her for the murder of a Dutch millionaire.

"We know you and your friends are responsible," said the Delhi police.

"But why?" she asked, while her parents stood by, stunned into silence. "He was a friend for two years. What motive could we have?"

"How should we know why you killed him? That is for you to reply. All we know is that you had dinner with this man. You left the house at midnight. Two hours later the servant found him in the bathroom. Dead."

"But he was perfectly all right when we left him," whispered the girl.

"If he was all right, then what was the dead man doing in the bathroom, naked in front of the commode?" asked the senior police officer sternly.

"Naked on the commode!" exclaimed the girl's mother in horror.

"Not *on* the commode," corrected the officer. "In front of it. Fallen forward onto his knees and chin, holding a book in his left hand."

The young Indian woman abruptly took the interrogation into her own hands.

"Now look here! If I had wanted to kill my friend, I would not have bothered to undress him. And I certainly would not have put a book into his hand. Kindly tell me what he was reading at the time of his death."

The police, thrown off balance by this unexpected aggression, looked hurriedly through their notes, and passed the relevant page to the officer in charge.

The officer cleared his throat and read: "The deceased was on the bathroom floor with a volume in his left hand, opened to page thirty-nine. The title of the volume is as follows, *The Tibetan Book of the Dead.*"

"There you are!" said the Indian girl triumphantly. "Who would leave such incriminating evidence in their victim's hands?"

The police officer was not listening to the girl. He was peering at the note on the file. Finally, he looked up and asked, "Was this Dutch millionaire by any chance Hindu-minded?"

"He was very interested in our philosophy," confirmed the girl.

"I see," said the officer, and signaled his men out of the house. As he reached the door, he turned around and addressed himself to the young woman's parents.

"If the deceased was Hindu-minded," observed the officer morosely, "it is the probable cause of death."

2

The girl later told me that the Dutch millionaire had died of terminal cancer. Nevertheless, the Delhi police had made an accurate deduction. Philosophy can sometimes be as lethal as cancer.

A lot of people who claim to be Hindu-minded are rushing around the world killing or being killed in the name of philosophy. Some are drawn by the machismo of the mumbo, others come for the jeopardies of the jumbo, but whatever their claims to profundity, the mumbo jumbo looks like good old-fashioned fascism to the insider.

Unlike the realities of cancer, the fantasies of fascism give you a choice. Victimizing or getting victimized, being the leader or playing follow the leader. Or, as they say in the star systems of America, winning or losing. Unfortunately, human constellations have repeatedly shown that stellar mortals have a high mortality rate. And of late, our radar screens have been jammed with falling bodies.

3

Some of those falling bodies are rumored to have been caused by people describing themselves as the "execution squads" of the Anand Marg cult.

This cult, like many another spontaneous movement on the

subcontinent, bumbled along until the spoils got large enough to
fight over to the death. Then the wife of the guru, Sarkar,
denounced him.

Sarkar, an ex-minor bureaucrat from Calcutta, has evolved a
philosophy that is an uneasy amalgam of socialism and Kali
worship, and this has gained him a surprisingly large following,
not only in India, but all over the world, specifically and
inexplicably in Australia.

So the reverberations were somewhat seismic when his wife
suddenly and dramatically announced that he was no socialist
egalitarian, but a pervert who sodomized young boys, and who
had had a number of people ritually murdered.

Skulls and bones were unearthed from burial mounds in
villages the Anand Margis were known to have visited. The guru
and the leaders of his organization, the Avadhoots, who occupy
roughly the same position as the heads of cells of any current
underground movement, claimed that the wife's allegations were
a fantastic frame, made with the active collaboration of a
repressive government frightened by the social legislation demanded by the cult. The repressive government promptly jailed
Sarkar and several senior Avadhoots, and let it be known there
was a CIA presence behind the Anand Marg.

People claiming to be Anand Margis retaliated by compiling a
Death List of the Indians they would kill until the government
released their guru. Sarkar, in jail in the Eastern Indian state of
Bihar, denied all knowledge of these people who were function-
ing in his name. The "faithful" went ahead and knifed a couple
of Indian diplomats and fired point-blank at an Air India official
in Melbourne, anyway.

Finally the repressive government changed and the new
government decided to bring charges against Sarkar. While the
case was being reviewed, the Indian Prime Minister went to
Sydney to attend the Asian Commonwealth Prime Ministers'
Conference. To the intense embarrassment of Australia, some-

one bombed the hotel in which six heads of government were staying. Fortunately, the Prime Ministers were being feted aboard a ship in Sydney harbor at the time of the explosion. But it was an exciting moment for Southeast Asia and again, people professing to be Anand Margis claimed the kudos. Release Sarkar Now, read their message, and the Australian police began a manhunt for three people, believed to be American and Australian.

Back in Bihar, Sarkar was released. The police could not produce sufficient evidence to prove that Sarkar had been the force behind the killings around the world, or that the name of his organization—as Sarkar had consistently claimed—was not being used by other cults engaged in black magic, or political movements, to shield the murders they were performing for their own rites.

"Well, what do you think?" I asked a freelance photographer who had managed to get close to the Anand Marg, and now in fear had an unlisted telephone number. "Did Sarkar have anything to do with all this killing or not?"

"I don't know. When I visited their headquarters here they seemed a perfectly reasonable and helpful group of people. Fifty percent of them were Indian, the other half foreign. They showed me their brochures, the dispensaries they ran, the crèches for the babies of the poor, the community centers. Not just here, but all over the world. It was very impressive, believe me. They asked me how anyone doing this kind of work could commit murder."

The photographer had asked if he could photograph their religious ceremonies.

"This young Indian Avadhoot said to me, 'How will you take photographs at night?' I told him I'd bring my flashes. Then he laughed, 'Will your flashes protect you from fear?' I said I was too old to be frightened of the dark.

"He said, 'Not the dark. There will be a full moon. But what about fear of death?' So I said, 'Aren't you frightened by death, too?'

"He said, 'Oh no, we're used to death.' Then someone, I think a foreigner, made him shut up. Well, what do you think?"

I couldn't, so I asked him again about the CIA.

"Oh CIA, CIA, CIA. I don't know.

"I mean this is India, for godssake. How can a man incarcerated in some far-off jail in Bihar organize such elaborate terrorism all over the world? Yet someone must have helped these alleged Anand Margis get the hardware, trained them in the use of explosives, all that logistical stuff.

"Some people say it's the CIA. Some say it's the North Koreans. Some say it's the East German Intelligence people. A lot of people say these movements are ripe for infiltration, and that the real leaders take their instruction from the KGB. They say Moscow instructs the cult fanatics in terrorism and then, to discredit the Americans, spreads the rumor that it's part of a CIA plot.

"It's all completely insane. I wouldn't believe any of it if I hadn't had a couple of death threats myself."

I thought the whole thing pretty farfetched too.

Until I saw a picture in the papers of the ex-Grand Master of chess, the Russian expatriate Korchnoi, doing meditation and yoga techniques with a white woman and a white man in the Philippines during the endless chess tournament between himself and a fellow Russian, Karpov.

The white man and the white woman had described themselves to the press as members of the Anand Marg cult and claimed to possess hidden strengths. Their claim was widely accepted. In fact the Australian Government took it so seriously that it was trying to extradite Korchnoi's two yoga teachers to assist inquiries about a case of alleged murder in Australia.

Korchnoi believed that Karpov's trainer, a senior member of the KGB who sat in the second row of the audience, was using the highly secret techniques in mind control developed by the Soviet Union to take over his mind and force him to lose to the USSR chess contender, Karpov.

The self-professed Anand Margis maintained that they could teach Korchnoi to resist modern KGB mind-bending techniques by initiating him into the mind-control arts of ancient India.

More of that old black magic.
Mind control. Market control. Out of control.

4

I sat in sepulchral darkness with a lovely young Indian girl in a starched cotton sari, sipping iced water and lime. The gloom had been laid on by understanding restaurant proprietors to shield the indiscretions of college girls, who used the coffee bar to meet their admirers, from the prying eyes of passing relatives. My companion had recently stopped being one of those over-chaperoned college girls, and was now a journalist covering a trial in which charges of mass murder were being brought against a personable young man of Indo-European parentage.

"I go to the courts every day, but the magistrate and the police won't let us talk to Sobhraj. I managed to get a photograph of him last week when he was coming out of the court. I just yelled, 'Charles! Charles! Look at me!' He turned around and I have a beautiful picture of him smiling. I'm thinking of blowing it up into a poster."

"Why?"

175

"Well, I know it's silly. The man has killed God knows how many people. But he's so good-looking. He has such sad eyes, and such an innocent face. He looks like an angel."

The man who she was describing so lyrically was being arraigned for the attempted murder of an entire French tour group. Sobhraj had wanted to rob them. To facilitate his theft he had drugged their drinks as they sat down to dine in the hotel dining room. The drug had not been everything that the chemist promised, it had taken effect sooner than Sobhraj had anticipated. The French tour group began dropping like flies in the dining room instead of in the decent privacy of their bedrooms. And Charles Sobhraj, wanted for murder in Bangkok, Malaysia, Nepal, Indonesia, and India, murders he had always performed with a nubile young female accessory or two, had at last been captured.

As the handcuffs were locked to his wrists, the debonair Sobhraj congratulated the Delhi police on being the ones to catch him.

The prosecution was asking for the maximum penalty anyway. Despite his good looks and his good manners, they wanted Sobhraj out of circulation.

Another Indian journalist, a man with dandruff on his shoulders and deep tobacco stains on his fingers, ran his hands nervously through his hair.

"I don't know what sort of chemistry the man possesses. But the terrible nature of his crimes and the fact that he's up for the death penalty, women seem to find this magnetically attractive. Not just our women. There was a girl here from *Paris Match*, a supposedly hard-bitten French journalist. Even she ended up with a serious crush on this madman."

Bloodlust. The killer and the sacrifice in one person. Like the Thugs of a hundred years ago, who killed their victims for Kali,

Goddess of Destruction, and kept the material spoils for themselves.

"Don't be such a romantic," said the journalist, and blew irritably at his hot tea. After sipping his tea for a moment he turned and looked at me.

"You know, last spring I went to Rishikesh on a story, to investigate the death of two nuns. The women had left their convent to follow some sadhu. Following the sadhu, they ended up fifteen hundred miles north of Madras, in the mountains above Rishikesh. When they came down from the mountains they used to talk to people in other ashrams and say how much they were learning from their guru. One of them wrote home and asked for thirty thousand francs to build an ashram for the guru. The money was forwarded to her and nobody ever heard from the nuns again.

"The Embassy and the police checked on the sadhu but he had disappeared without trace. When I investigated, I found that he called himself a Tantric. I think he must have gone in for ritual murder, because other followers were also missing. But only after they had contributed to the future ashram.

"He will reappear as a sadhu from a different valley, and more good and silly people will follow him to their death. Maybe there is some sense in your suggestion. Maybe the more men a person has killed, the greater his charisma. Otherwise wouldn't intelligent women find Sobhraj revolting instead of attractive?"

5

"You go to Anjuna you look for The Man. Lives behind the beach in Joe Banana's shack," a pair of eager American university students told me.

For all their cool, for all their weary been-on-the-road-a-year sophistication, they couldn't keep the hero worship out of their eyes or their words.

"He's a very heavy dude, I'm warning you. They say he's had three men killed already. I mean he *runs* Goa, man. The dope. The ladies. Everything. All the cops are in his pocket."

They had seen a lot of ugly things on the road from Europe to India, haphazard ugliness brought about by poverty or the hostility of the natives. Their admiration for their hero stemmed from their belief that he, a white man, had imposed his will on a foreign land, ruling it like a feudal kingdom.

"Course, he may not want to see you. He doesn't like strangers. That's only natural. You could be a spy or an informer, and he's got a big business to protect."

His business, they explained, was organizing other foreigners in a new game, daring them to match their wits and the cunning they claimed to have learned on the trail, against the customs officers and the narcotics agents of more civilized countries. With the added security of knowing that if they got busted, they would at least be jailed in their own countries and not in some savage Eastern prison, exposed to the random cruelties of an alien culture.

"He likes the ladies, though. When he's cruising he always has at least three women with him. One holds a big umbrella over his head to shade him from the sun. Two other chicks walk on either side of him, fanning him. It's really wild."

"So he may see you, on account of you're a woman."

"Yeah, but you'd better watch yourself. He's faster than greased lightning. When he's through with you, you'll either be carrying dope to Marseilles, or you'll disappear without trace."

An older Indian who had lain around the Goan beaches for years and knew The Man, held vehemently contradictory views to those expressed by the American students.

"Don't be silly. The Man, my foot. He's just another actor, and what a *ham*. He spreads these rumors that he's a killer to keep all his fans under control. He plays up to their fantasies and it's made him very rich."

The Indian sniffed contemptuously.

"A lot of them are broke, a real mess in one way or another, by the time they arrive in Anjuna. He strolls down the beach with all his props, the women, the fanning, the umbrella, and he buys passports or silver jewelry brought in from the Far East, or dope. Makes small-time smuggling deals, and always picks up women. I think it's the women more than anything else that have made him such a legend."

6

Two missions took me to Anjuna Beach in Goa. The Man. And a silver flute for the son of a Hollywood film lawyer. The American boy lay in a Bombay hospital with hepatitis, and a friend had asked me to visit him, on my way to Goa.

The thought of an Asian disease, contracted in India, administered to by native doctors, had shocked the boy and his family into re-establishing emotional and financial contact with each other after two years. The Road was too weird a concept for one side to describe and the other to understand, but disease was something over which ranks had to be closed.

The son, having made contact with family indulgence after his long absence, had now retreated into spoiled adolescence. He spent the long hours of convalescence in Bombay's most expensive hospital, painting his toenails green, insulting the doctors, refusing to use the hospital's delousing shampoo on the grounds that it would split the ends of his hair, and playing his bamboo flute on his private balcony, to the chagrin of the Russian diplomat who lay ill next door.

"Listen, could you do something for me in Goa?"

The boy was to have anything he wanted, and when he recovered he was to go home to Hollywood.

"There's a South American guy down there selling a beautiful silver flute. See, I only have this bamboo one and I taught myself to play it, but it doesn't have enough resonance. I really need a good instrument now, cause if I'm going to recover properly, bring my body back to the right rhythms, I don't just need the sounds, I need the right tone, the right vibrations. If you send harsh sounds out into the atmosphere, they come back and ZAP you."

The boy gave me elaborate instructions on how to conduct negotiations with the South American, so that I could obtain the flute at a price that the American boy considered reasonable. His idea of reasonable seemed rapacious to me, but then we older trading communities had become obsolescent: we could learn more from the mouths of babes coming in from the Americas than we had picked up from generations of market practice.

7

Anjuna Beach in Goa is an anthropologist's dream. It illustrates what people will keep and carry with them to the bitter end, long after they have lost their passports, their money, their virginity, their health, and often their sanity. There they are, still holding on to a plastic feeding bottle, two worn paperback thrillers, a box of American detergent, an opera hat, an extraordinary collection of items that have been clutched and carried five, eight, ten thousand miles across the face of the earth, to be displayed for sale by illogically destitute foreigners on the sands of an Indian beach.

The Flea Market was taking place in a grove of coconut palms, fifty yards from the sea. At the entrance to the grove was a large sign on which the municipal corporation banned nudity. In deference to the sign, and its implication of a fine, the men were moving around in loincloths, the women in strips of cloth tied around their hips and their breasts. From time to time these were removed and the Indians gawked appreciatively. Anjuna Beach had become to the Indians what the burning ghats were to the foreigners, mostly a place to watch others lose their dignity.

Six or seven hundred barters were taking place, over goods displayed on the rich red earth of the grove. Above, the coconut palms stretched sixty feet into the baked blue sky. It was difficult to locate a South American flute seller. I looked for a clue— something silver shining in the sun, someone making music, anything. But there were too many acts going on around me.

Two men were sitting on the ground in front of a torn red scarf on which they had spread their goods—a pair of gray terylene trousers and a water thermos. Over them stood a Goan couple who looked like they didn't have much money, the man perhaps a clerk from the local post office. The men in loincloths were leaning into each other, their eyes closed against the sun. The Goans were trying to get their attention. Finally one of the vendors opened an eye and asked in a broad Birmingham accent,

"What do you lot want, then?"

The clerk indicated that he would like to look at the trousers.

"Have you got two hundred rupees on you, you birk?" said the man.

The clerk and his wife were horrified.

"Two *hundred* rupees?" they asked in unison, visions of impossible extravagance in their eyes.

"Too steep, huh?" jeered the other man, his eyes still shut.

"What do you think this is? A charity show?"

The wife reached down to pick up the trousers. The man with the Birmingham accent slapped her hand away.

"Don't touch the goods if you don't have the money, missus. These are high-quality trousers all the way from Marks and bleeding Spencers. Can't have your sort leaving dirty marks on them."

The woman jumped back, grabbed her husband's elbow, and the couple went off muttering about the price and the foreigners.

The Birmingham man yawned and looked at me.

"Don't suppose you've got two hundred rupees either, have you, love? Just a tourist come to look at the cheeky men. Well, we hate to disappoint."

With those words, he flipped up his loincloth. I looked at the man and sternly asked if he knew of a South American trying to sell a silver flute. His companion's eyes opened. A connection, however tenuous, had been established. That made me friend, not enemy.

"Try asking the Indian," he said pointing at a tree at the far end of the coconut grove.

"Any particular Indian?" I enquired.

"Not an Indian Indian," he said impatiently. "The Brazilian one."

Getting to the other side of the grove meant picking one's way past the people and their possessions on the ground, and past the Indian snake charmers to whom a crowd meant business even at a barter bazaar.

An old man with grizzled hair was waving a cobra in the face of a tanned and plump brunette curled in a fetal position on the sand. The brunette wouldn't open her eyes. She lay there repeating,

"Piss off, willya, asshole. I wanna sleep. Just lemme alone, willya?"

She had a strip of cloth tied around her waist and another strip stretched inadequately across her large breasts. In front of her was her stall—four cartons of Swiss breakfast food, stuck crookedly into the sand. She had brought them all the way from the West, and they now represented her last bit of legal tender. She didn't seem too preoccupied with selling them.

The sun was throwing dappled shadows over her Rubenesque limbs. The old man squatted beside her. He pulled his biggest snake out of the basket and held it over her head, inches from her face.

"Look, lady. Nice snake. Make danger. Sexy."

The girl opened her eyes and saw the snake darting its tongue in and out above her face. She opened her mouth and let out a long thin scream of terror. Her limbs jerked stiffly, her breasts fell out of their covering. The old man looked at her lasciviously. Then he laughed, spat a red streak of paan spittle over her body, and put the snake back in its basket.

At the far end of the market was a solitary palm tree. It stretched into the cloudless sky. A youth leaned against the tree, his skin a deep brown, his black hair falling straight and thick to his shoulders, completely naked.

I had by this time rejoined the Goan grandee who had accompanied me to the Flea Market, curious to see what had happened to the beach that had belonged to his family in the days of the Portuguese. The grandee and myself halted involuntarily, rooted to the spot by the sheer beauty of the youth.

His perfectly shaped torso dipped into narrow hips, then elongated out into long powerful legs. His hands hung loosely at his waist. One hand held a silver flute. If he had put the flute to his lips he could have been the God Krishna, freezing the vulgarity and the chaos around him in one moment of perfect synthesis.

But he didn't, and we moved toward him.

He looked at us expectantly and said nothing. In front of him were his wares, two books on a piece of cloth spread before his naked feet. The Goan grandee bent down to look at the titles.

"A Bible and a missal?" asked the grandee, puzzled. "Now who on this beach would dream of buying these?"

"Maybe he'll sell his flute instead," I suggested. I turned to the youth who had shown no signs of being able to follow our conversation.

"Is your flute for sale?" I enquired.

He smiled and didn't answer. Then the grandee asked him the same question in Portuguese. The boy's eyes lit up. He shook his head vigorously. The grandee pointed to the books at the boy's feet. The boy began to speak. After a couple of minutes, unable to understand the boy's Portuguese, I asked what was happening.

"He was studying for the priesthood in Brazil. He doesn't think he can be a priest now, so he's selling the Bible and the missal."

"Why can't he be a priest? Is he bored with the idea?"

"Because he's in a state of mortal sin."

"Why doesn't he confess it? I mean, if he still wants to be a priest. He hasn't actually killed anyone or anything, has he?"

The grandee ignored me and proceeded to have a lengthy conversation with the boy. The boy picked up the Bible and pointed out something. Then he reached under the cloth, pulled out his passport and showed that to the grandee.

"Ask him about the flute," I said.

The grandee paid no attention and continued to talk to the boy. Finally, they embraced. My friend took my arm and led me firmly away.

"What about the flute?"

"He doesn't have to sell it anymore."

"Why not?"

"Because he's got his passport back."

"Was it lost?"

"No, he sold it. Then he found his embassy wouldn't give him another one. He went out on the streets and found himself a protector. A Dutchman who deals in passports. He bought the passport and flute back for the boy."

"What did it cost?" I asked.

"Well, first he had to be the Dutchman's whore. And then, he had to be a courier. He has to make three more trips smuggling drugs to Amsterdam to raise enough money to return to Brazil."

The grandee paused and said in disgust,

"Why don't we close places like this down, for godssake?"

Three months later the authorities did just that. They thought too many Indians were buying smuggled tape recorders.

8

On our way out of the Flea Market we saw a large, well-built man coming toward us, flanked by young and scantily dressed women. The Man.

He wore three silver belts around his torso. The third belt hung low on his hips. From it swung a long silver knife, which dangled between his buttocks. His bare arms were tattooed with multicolored serpents, which rippled up and down as he flexed his muscles.

He looked at me long and hard. Then he turned his face sideways,

"I look like Chief Crazy Horse, no?"

Yes.
He was in the wrong Indies, but he had the right act.

XII

.

BEING HINDU MEANS NEVER HAVING TO SAY YOU'RE SORRY

I

"I left the ashram because it's so corrupt. The guru never stops playing favorites."

"I thought this ashram was going to show me the way. No more politics. Only philosophy and salvation. I should get so lucky. There's more politics in one Indian ashram than in the whole of the Western Hemisphere!"

"It's rather sick really. The people who are rich get closer to the guru than those who are poor."

"In the end I stopped caring about guru contact. I just got tired of having to do all the dirty jobs, while the rich powerful guys sat around being holy."

Disenchantment in the cloisters.
Is it justified?
Can the gurus be dismissed as con men, manipulating their way to great fortunes? Or is the plot in fact thicker than cash?

2

No one heeded Ravi Shankar when he pleaded with his audiences: "Get high on the music, it is enough!"

Nothing was enough to those who had heard the sirens scream Turn On, Tune In, Expand your Mind.

Alas, the mind can be expanded until it bursts, and when it does there stands an Indian parental type saying, Oh yes, this is a common mind-expansion problem, bursting. It has been going on in our country for about four thousand years. Why not come to my ashram? I will heal your mind if you give me your soul.

But you don't have psychology, says the West.

Then what is meditation, asks the professional guru, if not a continuous examination of states of mind? What is Maya but an analysis of fantasy and illusion? Come into my parlor and you will learn more than you ever dreamed.

How about the sexual revolution? asks the Occident.

Promiscuity is no revolution, answers the guru. Sexual truth is this statue of the Buddha in the lotus position, copulating with the Goddess of Energy.

The ordinary tourist pays an ordinary price for his bronze conversation piece, the Buddha in the Bangkok Squat, and Mick Jagger shows up in Katmandu to see if he can do it too—Gimme a Honky Tonk Man.

The metaphysical tourist wants that smile on the Buddha's face, the serenity of the cosmic orgasm. To him the novelty specialty guru says,

If you're real good
I'll make you feel good.

And being real good can mean anything from paying to killing
to dying.

3

The complaints of the disciples who flee from the venality of
the ashrams is that in some sense the guru has broken the law.
The law of the superhuman.

The disciples tell the guru,

"It's not fair. We have been sitting at your feet all these
months doing everything you tell us to do. You make laws for us
but none for yourself."

The guru replies,

"I make rules for you. What have rules got to do with the
Law?"

The disciples have come from a profoundly dogmatic culture.
With dogma like mathematics. Beginning with the Zero, in
order to proceed.

India says, Trade you the Void for the Zero, and the Western
optimist says, Sure, is that all it takes to be Enlightened? India
does not remind optimists that she conceptualized the Zero in
order to make infinity tolerable. Imagine a universe without
mathematical definition. Or put another way, look on the
immeasurable.

Dogma like causality.

The guru says,

"You haven't been listening. I told you there is no cause and no effect. No past and no future. Everything is simultaneous."

The disciples reply in chorus.

"Yeah, we can dig that. You're saying, Be Here Now!"

The irritated guru shouts, "You are here now. Do you understand what it means to be forever in the present? It means you are denied regret. And prohibited from hope."

The disciples say, "Wow. This must be the mystic East."

4

Jung had the good sense to be cautious about India. He said he had met many Occidentals in his travels through the subcontinent who thought they were living in India. Jung maintained that they were in fact living in bottles of Western air, protected from India by objectivity, causality, and all the other intellectual apparatus of the West. He went on to say, "It is quite possible that India is the real world and that the white man lives in a madhouse of abstractions." Emphasizing that without those abstractions the white man would disintegrate in India.

Jung got it right except for one omission. The Indian is no better at handling reality than anyone else, but we live closer to it so we have to take more elaborate evasive action.

Hindu thought is without dogma, and dogged by Dharma.

Dharma means no distinction between chaos and order, accepting good and evil as indivisible, witnessing simultaneous continuity as the moral order, being as a process of endless becoming. And yet to act. It means you cannot follow the Law. You are the Law.

If the white man lives in a madhouse of abstractions, then we live in a madhouse of distractions. But we give our distractions philosophical names, such as: Bhakti Yoga, the meditation of adoration. Hatha Yoga, the meditation of physical endurance Tantra Yoga, the meditation of the senses. Guru Yoga, enlightenment through the Teacher. Reincarnation, enlightenment through rebirth.

Over and over again when Dharma is acknowledged to be too harsh, our meditations and our spiritual techniques have degenerated into payola systems, and those systems are used to buy time against Time. And we have a philosophical name for payola systems, too. We call them Leela, the meditation of the practical joke.

Like the practical jokes being perpetrated daily in the ashrams of India.

5

The disenchanted disciples of the ashrams say,

"How come our guru's got a solid golden toilet seat? Does he shit gold or something? He doesn't? Well, if he's an ascetic and above earthly desire and stuff, what is he doing with a golden toilet seat?"

The guru replies,

"Those things are Maya. They are mere illusion."

The disciples say, "Come on, Guru. Golden toilet seats are corruption. We hope you feel guilty about all this religious bull you're laying on us."

That's when the corrupt guru counsels his disciples to forget about guilt and rules and toilet seats, and contemplate the Law.

6

A Zen Buddhist priest in Japan, revered as a National Treasure for his wisdom, explained the hazards of being a Teacher to one of his disciples, a friend of mine. The Zen Master had brooded on the Buddha's dilemma.

The Buddha had said, "God is Nothing!" and been elevated to divinity.

The more the Buddha explained the Void, the faster his disciples rushed to fill the Void with the Buddha. Groupies hate a vacuum. In the end the Buddha survived. He died. But even at the moment of his death, his disciples were busily planning his monument. How did the Enlightened One wish to be buried? The Enlightened One picked up two empty alms bowls and placed one over the other. This gesture his disciples promptly immortalized into the monumental Buddhist stupas, which are, to this day, a must for the discerning tourist. The Buddha's point with the alms bowls was simple, he was covering emptiness with emptiness, but the devout wouldn't have it.

7

The American poet Wallace Stevens reminded the West that the last illusion is disillusion. The Indian guru reminds the Westerner what lies beyond the last illusion.

"But you're saying I'm God," say the disciples, "That I'm responsible."

"That's right," answers the guru.

"No. That's not fair. You're the guru. You're supposed to tell me what to do. I'm sorry but I can't handle the Law."

The guru clears his throat and points out: "But, nonetheless, you are the Law. You cannot receive mercy. So it's no good being sorry."

The guru has revealed the last move in the Hindu end game. He beams with the pleasure of a man who has fulfilled his Karma as a Teacher. He waits to be showered with rose petals by grateful ashram graduates. But the distressed devotees are rushing for the exit.

"What's happening?" asks the guru.

"We have this headache," say the disillusioned disciples. "Maybe it's the climate or the food or something. We think we'll go home for a while. How do we leave?"

"That's an interesting question," says the guru, with a smile. "You're the tourists. You find out."

XIII

.

OM IS WHERE
THE ART IS

I

The whims of the West were so easily translated into revelation by India. But revelation comes expensive in the East. Kipling did point out that India is the grim stepmother of the world, and the mythology of India illustrates over and over again that it is one thing to feel playful, it is quite another thing to sit down at the table.

In many Indian temples, the idol in front of which you place your incense and your fruit and your marigolds has a reverse image, the image of the profane. This image is not to be looked upon unless you are prepared to forego the securities of the clichés of the sacred. Those who dare and who do not self-destruct are sometimes referred to as "realized souls."

What they have realized is that you get no points for good faith in a game of dirty poker.

Even the great Pandavas discovered that although the dice were loaded against them, they couldn't get up. The game was only a game, but the ante was for real. After they had thrown everything into the pot, their money, their country, their wife, and their royal line, they had to roll the dice one more time. On that throw they lost their liberty, and faced the choice of slavery or exile.

2

We still confront that choice in India because of something in the air. It is coming in from the West and telling us that while there are no free lunches, Utopia is possible. Poverty, disease and death are not reality. They are inefficiency. If we work hard enough and fast enough we will conquer the first two, and any minute now there will be a breakthrough in genetic engineering, which will allow everyone to view death as superstition.

For us to reprogram ourselves, for us to fully grasp that life is not about doing time but about making time, means that we have to dump most of our philosophical perceptions overboard and accept the imperatives of history, hoping we will not become exiles in our own land.

And there in the lifeboats, fighting to grab those perceptions, are the very people who told us to get rid of the ballast and be free.

This is known as mythological osmosis, and as an Indian writer has pointed out, it is possible that in the not too distant future if the Indian wants to learn about India he will have to consult the West, and if the West wants to remember how they were, they will have to come to us.

This is also known as rock and roll.

3

There are those who still regard the compass as more than a bauble and persist in asking total strangers, "Where's home?" and "Who's Om?" They may be comforted to learn that their dilemma is not unique.

A century ago Nietzsche was asking in italics,

"Will it be said of us one day that we too,
steering westward, hoped to reach an India,
but that it was our fate to be wrecked against infinity?"

To the anxious, on both sides of the dark water, I would like to raise a toast: A small cheer for fear.

It's harder to applaud the confident ones who as the Indian cynic says, "Go from zero to hero."

Those who have passed beyond fear can't hear.

A Selected List of Fiction Available from Minerva

While every effort is made to keep prices low, it is sometimes necessary to increase prices at short notice. Mandarin Paperbacks reserves the right to show new retail prices on covers which may differ from those previously advertised in the text or elsewhere.

The prices shown below were correct at the time of going to press.

☐	7493 9026 3	**I Pass Like Night**	Jonathan Ames	£3.99
☐	7493 9121 9	**Evening Wolves**	Joan Chase	£5.99
☐	7493 9808 6	**To Kill a Mockingbird**	Harper Lee	£5.99
☐	7493 9907 4	**Pinocchio in Venice**	Robert Coover	£5.99
☐	7493 9046 8	**Love in the Days of Rage**	Lawrence Ferlinghetti	£3.99
☐	7493 9027 1	**The Lover of Horses**	Tess Gallagher	£3.99
☐	7493 9032 8	**Years From Now**	Gary Glickman	£4.99
☐	7493 9189 8	**Paper Products**	James Hall	£5.99
☐	7493 9099 9	**The Sporting Club**	Thomas McGuane	£4.99
☐	7493 9132 4	**Bicycle Days**	John Burnham Schwartz	£4.99
☐	7493 9072 7	**Leaving Brooklyn**	Lynne Sharon Schwartz	£4.99
☐	7493 9957 0	**The Joy Luck Club**	Amy Tan	£5.99
☐	7493 9141 3	**Vineland**	Thomas Pynchon	£4.99
☐	7493 9155 3	**Grapes of Wrath**	John Steinbeck	£5.99

All these books are available at your bookshop or newsagent, or can be ordered direct from the publisher. Just tick the titles you want and fill in the form below.

Mandarin Paperbacks, Cash Sales Department, PO Box 11, Falmouth, Cornwall TR10 9EN.

Please send cheque or postal order, no currency, for purchase price quoted and allow the following for postage and packing:

UK including
BFPO

£1.00 for the first book, 50p for the second and 30p for each additional book ordered to a maximum charge of £3.00.

Overseas
including Eire

£2 for the first book, £1.00 for the second and 50p for each additional book thereafter.

NAME (Block letters) ....

ADDRESS ....

....

☐ I enclose my remittance for ....

☐ I wish to pay by Access/Visa Card Number

Expiry Date